Everybody
Has an Angel

Everybody Has an Angel

ANSELM GRUEN

Translated by
SHARON THERESE NEMETH

A Crossroad Book
The Crossroad Publishing Company
New York

First published in English in the U.S.A. in 2000 by
The Crossroad Publishing Company
481 Eighth Avenue, New York, NY 10001

Original edition: *Jeder Mensch hat einen Engel*
Published by Herder Verlag, Freiburg im Breisgau, 1999

Printed in the United States of America

Library of Congress Cataloging-in-Publication Data

Gruen, Anselm.
    [Jeder Mensch hat einen Engel. English]
    Everybody has an angel / Anselm Gruen ; translated by Sharon
Therese Nemeth.
      p. cm.
    Includes bibliographical references.
    ISBN 0-8245-1861-6 (alk. paper)
    1. Angels – Biblical teaching. I. Title.
  BS680.A48 G7813 2000
  235$'$.3 – dc21

                            00-009448

1 2 3 4 5 6 7 8 9 10   06 05 04 03 02 01 00

Contents

Introduction

Belief in a personal guardian angel is widespread in many religions. The early church shared a belief with Jewish tradition that God gave each person an angel, who accompanied him or her on the passage from birth to death and beyond into paradise. Up until several years ago this belief was made light of by academic theologians as a childlike idea that had nothing to do with the truths of Christianity. According to a poll by *Focus* magazine, a surprisingly high number of people believe in a personal guardian angel. Belief in angels is apparently more credible for most people today than belief in God and in Jesus Christ.

In the New Age movement it has become popular to speak about visible angels, who stay by each of us teaching us important lessons helpful for mastering life. The physical appearance of angels exercises a wide fascination. In my view, however, the New Age movement places the emphasis all too often on the out-of-the-ordinary. Nevertheless, through its angel books, angel conventions, and angel seminars, people's curiosity awakes in a secular world to something that goes beyond the banality of everyday life. Through angels, mystery enters lives that are often lived out superficially.

When I write that everybody has an angel, I am taking the biblical tradition as my basis. I look at biblical stories of angels who come to the aid of people and show them the right direction to go. I have chosen twenty-four stories that describe in beautiful images how an angel intervenes in a hopeless situation, watches over and protects, and opens a person's eyes to the path that leads to life. In these angel stories it becomes apparent that the angels never abandon those they are leading in any situation, but are constant companions along the way, offering protection and comfort just when the feeling of being isolated with fear is the greatest.

I also write about the angel each of us has from a therapeutic interest. In many conversations people have told me that the idea of a personal guardian angel at their side has helped them to take control of their lives. The image of the guardian angel was especially helpful to them as children. The angel who accompanied them was just as real as the doll they played with or the teddy bear they took to bed with them. People often tell me their life story concentrating solely on the hurt that they have experienced. It is undoubtedly important that we look at the injuries that caused us pain as children or later on in our lives. However, I meet many people who focus *only* on their hurt. New methods are continually promoted on how to confront these early childhood injuries. Constantly trying to discover new wounds seems to be almost an addiction. Here the idea is helpful that not only were these people at the mercy of those who hurt them but rather that an angel was also standing by their side protecting them, and leading them to a place where they could breathe a sigh of relief and experience healing. Instead of repeatedly opening the "wounds of unlovedness" (Peter Schellenbaum), it would often be better for us to look for the tracks the angels have left in our lives. "Angel tracks" are what I call the beneficial and healing traces that can be found in every person's life. I discover them when I ask myself where I felt happy as a child, where I was able to lose myself, and where I was completely absorbed in my games. Where were my favorite places? What did I do there? What did I most like to play? Where was I completely in my element? When I follow these tracks I come to realize that I was not always at the mercy of sick and hurtful parents but rather that an angel accompanied me as a child. The angel made it possible for me to go on, despite injuries and hardships, and to stay healthy and find my own path in life.

The idea that every child has an angel can relieve the strain on parents. Many worry excessively about whether they are raising their children properly, whether negative influences from outside are leading them astray, or whether the hurt that they can unconsciously cause their children might damage them forever. While such worries and fears are certainly founded, I meet parents who, through psychological books, have become completely unsure of their own abilities. They want to do everything perfectly and take pains to follow exactly the advice that is given. However, they stop trusting their own feelings anymore. This causes contact with their children to become even more complicated. It can even happen that by avoiding any possibility of hurting their children, they end up wounding them more than parents who follow their natural instincts. The idea that every child has an angel can free parents from their excessive worry. In spite of the limitations of parents and their shortcomings in child rearing, children can grow up healthy because angels are watching over and leading them.

This book, however, is aimed not only at parents, but also at those who are looking at their own childhood, perhaps dealing with it in therapy or spiritual counseling, to confront repression or injuries that prevent them from really living. Sometimes these people are desperate. They have already thought often about their childhood and spoken to others about it. Perhaps they have even tried to work out everything that was burdening them. But they can go only so far with knowledge alone. The recognition of where and when they were hurt does not heal their wounds. On the contrary, many seek continually to find out more about the pain that they experienced in life, rubbing salt in their wounds and tearing off the scabs again. It is also important for these people to follow the tracks the angels have left in their lives. They were not only at the mercy of an alcoholic father or a depressed mother during their childhood. Their lives were not only influenced by negative messages such as, "You'll never succeed in life. You're a burden to me. It would be better if you'd never been born." An angel was also at their side, making it possible for them to experience another environment where they could feel at home, free from the negative influences around them, and where they could sense healing and wholeness. Getting in touch with these angel tracks can be just as healing as a critical examination of our wounds. When we identify the tracks the angels have left in our lives, we will also be able to discover the angel who is at our side now and who wants to lead us to life just as it did in the past.

Based on the angel appearances and encounters in the Bible, I would like to look at how angels place their protective hands on children, and on every person, and what effect angels have on us. In doing this it is not my aim to present an exegetical interpretation of these biblical passages, but rather to present a descriptive interpretation of our personal experience. Angels can be fittingly described only in images. The Bible shows us how this is done. If we allow ourselves to enter into the images of the Bible, we will discover more about the angels who help us than we will through theological speculation. However, I would also like to touch briefly on the theological and psychological positions regarding a fitting way to speak about angels, in part to separate myself from some of the exaggerated viewpoints about angels that are propagated today.

A Fitting Way to Speak about Angels

Much is said about angels in New Age circles today. It is apparent that people yearn to see and experience the supernatural world. In the New Age world the idea of angels has been influenced by pagan gods and goddesses and shaped by the experiences of mediums and clairvoyants. Angels are placed in the astral world and possess a nonmaterial nature. In the early church such concrete ideas about angels already held a fascination for people. So the author of the letter to the Colossians warned the first Christians: "Let no one disqualify you, insisting on self-abasement and worship of angels, taking his stand on visions, puffed up without reason by his sensuous mind" (Col. 2:18). Apparently the heretics, whom the letter to the Colossians warns of, practiced an angel cult and felt superior to the Christians who just followed Jesus Christ. This feeling of superiority is echoed in many New Age works, which express the wish to have more knowledge than people are capable of possessing. Because of this, it is necessary to speak about angels as is fitting in the Christian tradition.

Theological Approaches

Angels have been much neglected in the theology of the past thirty years. Theology tells us that although the Bible presumes the existence of angels, it does not invent it. Angels simply belonged to the worldview of that time, which the Bible also uses to speak about God and God's effect on people. But angels actually had no further significance. Christian theology managed just as well without speaking about angels. In contrast to this critical position, the history of theology and Christian dogma shows that church tradition views angels as creatures of God. This means that they are created by God in the same way that humans are and stand in the service of God. And if angels are creatures, "then they have to be recognizable with normal human cognitive power" (Vorgrimler 31). They are spiritually personal powers and forces. Therefore, according to the teachings of the church an angel is more than merely an image for the healing and loving closeness of God. Angels are forces that possess an inner strength. And they have a mission for humans. As spiritual-personal creatures they are necessarily related to the human spirit and personality and have a direct influence on these areas. This means that they should be seen primarily in their connection to people and less as isolated creatures.

According to St. Augustine the word "angel" designates a mission rather than a being. An angel is God's emissary, through which God sends a message to people, accompanies them, or inspires them. The angel can come to us in a person, in a dream, or in our soul. The place in which an angel can be experienced is the human heart. The conviction of the Bible, shared by the church fathers, is that a person can see and experience an angel again and again. These encounters are described vividly. A deeper penetration into the being and workings of angels and the human curiosity to possess an intimate knowledge of them are rightfully rejected by the church.

If we take the teachings of the church seriously, then we can rightfully speak about angels through whom God shows us his closeness and affects us personally. God uses the created energy of angels to express himself. This could be psychic energy — the helping powers in our soul. It could be the prayers of other people, and it could also be the loving intercession of those whom we have loved who are now deceased. Vorgrimler rightfully asks: "Should such psychic energies be considered meaningless? It cannot be wrong to trust in God's protection as conveyed through such protective forces" (Vorgrimler 105). If angels are created spiritual beings, then they can come to us through their own spiritual power, in other people, and in dreams, to interpret life and affect us in a healing and helping way. In this way angels make God's closeness to us tangible. God's loving closeness surrounds me as created reality through the angel, thus becoming for me a concrete experience. I don't just have to believe in God's closeness; it can also be experienced, for example, as a thought that suddenly flashes through my mind. In accordance with Christian tradition it is legitimate to say that an angel inspired me with this thought.

The Bible often speaks about angels in connection with dreams. In a dream an angel speaks to me and God's message becomes concrete. A woman told me that she could never believe that God loved her. When she read or heard in a sermon that she was God's beloved daughter, it had no meaning for her, as if it did not apply to her. But then she dreamed that a voice spoke to her saying, "You are my beloved daughter, in whom I am well pleased." In a dream the word of God became an inner reality. She no longer had only to believe that it was true, because she experienced the word of God as reality. An angel conveyed this message to her, indeed, in such a way that she could experience it personally.

If angels are created reality, they can also come to us as a spiritual force that surrounds us, or they can take the form of a person. A person can become an angel for us. Other people are not essentially angels, but at one time or another can become one for me. Through another person I experience God's helping and loving closeness. A created reality is also the inner light that sometimes flashes through our mind or an image that surfaces inside us. And a created reality is the idea of the angel who surrounds me — the image of a shining spiritual being. We often cannot differentiate whether these images are dreams or visions, or if an angel can indeed be seen with human eyes. This is, however, not a crucial factor. Whether dreams, visions, or visible spiritual beings, these are always encounters where something happens that is perceived by people as an angel — a messenger of God. We are able to experience God's healing and protective closeness directly through an angel.

We do not need to believe in angels. Angels are not a subject of faith. We can just believe in God. But through angels belief in God's love can become concrete and multiply. Angels can be experienced. They connect our world with the world of God. Through angels God enters into our everyday reality. And because of this it is good for us to speak about them. God always remains the utterly Other, inconceivable and unnameable; God is the absolute mystery that we can never fully comprehend. In the angels God shows us his closeness in a human way. Because of this we can speak about angels. But we should always do this in connection with God and not — in the New Age manner — purely out of interest in the unusual. Angels are messengers of

God. They show us the way to God. They open our eyes to the mystery of God. They create the connection between heaven and earth, between God and human beings. They climb down Jacob's ladder from heaven to fix God's message in our hearts.

Psychological Approaches

The Protestant pastoral psychologist Ellen Stubbe addresses the thoughts of English child psychologist Donald W. Winnicott in order to find a fitting way to speak about angels today. Winnicott speaks about "transcendental objects" and "transcendental phenomena." He differentiates between an outer and inner world in children. The outer world is determined by the parents, as well as by what the child comes into contact with and finds interesting. The inner world is the child's own imagination. Winnicott also talks about the existence of a "third dimension." This is a "middle area of experience, which is influenced by the inner reality as well as the outside world. It is an area that cannot be held in question" (Stubbe 61), an oasis where the child can rest, and where the child is helped to connect the inner and outer realities. A stuffed toy, a doll, or some other thing serves as a transitional object, helping the child to overcome a fear of the dark or other unfamiliar feelings. This transitional object enables the child to sense protection and security even when the mother, for whom the object often serves as a substitute, is not there. Bringing the inner and outer worlds into harmony is a continual human process, according to Winnicott. From childhood on we are helped in doing this through direct contact with the middle area of experience: for children this is in games, where they can live out their fantasies and imagination. For adults the middle area is transferred to art and religion.

This is the area where Stubbe, in fitting language, places angels. The idea of the angel helps both children and adults to keep their identity intact. Children as well as adults are threatened with losing their individual identity. When children pray to their angel, they subconsciously sense that it holds their fragile identity together, because they feel whole and precious. Angels, says Stubbe, enter situations that are threatened by inner and outer disintegration, and their effect is directed toward "integration and wholeness" (Stubbe 276). The psychological function of the angel is "first as a support for self-development, and second to safeguard the existing self" (263).

But angels not only form the self; they also bring us into contact with God. This is because a child is more likely to speak about angels than about God. It can also be easier for adults to speak about angels than God, who often seems so far away and abstract as not to be experienced directly. In the same way as the inner and outer realities, angels also belong to the middle area that connects heaven with earth and tangible everyday life with God. Through the idea of angels who stay by our side, God's healing and loving closeness becomes concrete for us. From the beginning, angels have opened a horizon of experience. I do not have to believe in angels; they are experienced and in their ambiguity remain in a place between imagination and reality. We call people who help us angels. We also sense that deep inside of us an angel prevails, who opens our eyes to true reality, who keeps our threatened self-identity intact, and who accompanies us over the threshold of death and into the light of eternity.

The psychology of C. J. Jung offers us further insight into

a fitting way to speak about angels. For children, angels often serve as an image that substitutes for absent parents. The idea of the angel helps children to feel secure in spite of their situation. Jung believes that children not only experience their tangible mother and father, but also carry archetypal images of a mother and father within them. These archetypal ideals are necessary for a child to experience feelings such as security and protection despite a negative parental background. Through these images, which often take the form of an angel in children, a child has a sense of the loving and concerned mother. Jung does not write about the existence of angels, but only about their reality in the psyche: "If angels are indeed *something,* then they are the person-ified envoys of the subconscious expressing themselves" (13:91). Angels convey to children the feeling of a deeper sense of se-curity than the parents can give. They let children know that another power holds its protective hand over them. This calms a child's deep-seated fears. Just as fairy tales bring children in contact with life-giving sources in the subconscious, angels serve a similar function. Jung credits angels with having a significant influence on consciousness. If we do not admit the message of the angel into our consciousness, then the energy flows into the subconscious "into the area of affectivity, specifically in the sphere of emotional or biological drives. This results in emo-tional eruptions, irritability, mood swings, and sexual arousal through which the consciousness habitually suffers fundamen-tal disorientation" (13:91). For Jung, the angel represents "an opposing pole to the subjective ego." It stands for "a part of the objective psyche" (11:660). Human beings are not only ego; we are also influenced by the world of the subconscious. Destruc-tive powers can come from the subconscious that lead to such atrocities as those committed during the Third Reich. However, angels also arise from the subconscious, conveying to us a sense of "beauty, goodness, wisdom, and grace" (11:660). Experiencing the heights and depths of human nature entitles us to speak about angels, according to Jung. Jung describes angels as "spiritual guiding powers of the soul," "archetypal symbols with a spiritual energy that can affect the human ego and consciousness in a frightening or a healing way" (Hark 117).

Against this background of theological and psychological approaches to a fitting way to speak about angels, I would like to present some images of angels as described to us in the Bible. In doing so I will focus on the mission of angels rather than on angels as creatures. Above all I want to look at how angels give us impulses along the path to our self-realization: to start off, to continue on, to get up after we fall, and not to give up. I do this based on the assumption that every person has an angel. However, I dispense with describing this angel further. Speaking about angels always requires room for fantasy and creativity. It requires a place for trust, shaped by the experience of healing closeness. People, as well as God, can unlock such a place of trust. In this place of fundamental trust, which reaches the dimensions of heaven, we can speak about angels in a fitting way. To do this, images are necessary. Only images can express the essence of angels and how through them our lives become brighter and brighter.

1 The Guardian Angel

In the Gospel according to Matthew, Jesus says to his disciples:

> See that you do not despise one of these little ones; for I
> tell you that in heaven their angels always behold the face
> of my Father who is in heaven. (Matt. 18:10)

When he says "little ones," Jesus does not mean only children,
but also the unknown, unnoticed, simple people in the Christian community. Here Jesus says that each of these small and
often forgotten people has an angel who looks upon the face of
God. This Bible verse has led to the church teaching of a personal guardian angel. The idea of a guardian angel can be found
in many religions. In this instance, Jesus adopts the Jewish idea
but takes it a step further. While in Rabbinical Judaism guardian
angels are said to exist on earth and do not behold the face of
God, Jesus says that every person has a guardian angel who at
the same time looks upon God. Every person is under the special protection of God, who sends a personal emissary to each
one of us. The church fathers interpreted this verse to mean that
from birth every person has a guardian angel, a teaching that has
been perpetuated up to today.

What does this mean? The church is clearly convinced that
God places a guardian angel at every person's side. Some church
fathers even taught that angels play a role in a person's conception (Origen, Tertullian, Clement of Alexandria). An individual
does not exist without an angel, and this angel makes each per-

son complete. The church fathers attributed a guardian angel not only to each person, but to each nation, and even to individual communities. In the Book of Revelation the messages the visionary receives are directed to the angel of each respective community (Revelation 2).

Thus, every child has a guardian angel. Adults often tell me how important the idea of a guardian angel was to them in childhood. This angel gave them security in an uncertain world. Children have a natural sense for the reality of the angel. The French child analyst Françoise Doro relates in her memoirs how her daily life was determined by the bond she felt to her guardian angel. She lived together with her guardian angel as if it were beside her: "When I went to sleep I lay on only one side of the bed to leave room for my guardian angel to sleep next to me. I thought back over what had happened during the day, which, as usual, had ended as a disaster because I had supposedly done a lot of dumb things. Unfortunately, I didn't know how they happened or why I did them, which caused me to worry a lot" (Stubbe 58). She is completely convinced that her guardian angel has never abandoned her throughout her life. Every time she is looking for a parking place it comes to her aid. She says, "The child's guardian angel sleeps next to the child, but an adult's guardian angel is constantly keeping watch" (58).

Parents cannot guard every path their child takes. The more they want to control the actions of their children, the more fear and aggression they generate in them. Parents who want to control everything often have to experience the exact thing that they had dreaded most. Here the belief that a guardian angel protects the child from danger is helpful. But what good is this belief for parents when their child is hit by another child on the way home from school or when the child is even sexually abused? The guardian angel cannot be held responsible for everything that happens, nor can we place excessive demands on it. The things that we can manage ourselves are things we should do. Above all we should act wisely and be able to estimate accurately the reality of this world. A "middle area" still remains, however, that cannot be anticipated or planned according to rules. Because of this, it is helpful when parents entrust their children to a guardian angel. Doing this relieves them from the burden of their own worries. In spite of all of their worrying, parents cannot guarantee that their children will come home safely from school, or that they will not hurt themselves playing. Whoever tries to protect a child from every danger out of fear that something will happen, blinds the child to genuine dangers. Children have to test what they are capable of, and when they do, something can always happen; they can always underestimate their limitations. Trusting in the guardian angel and taking the necessary precautions must go hand in hand. We cannot explain why children fall prey to danger and lose their lives in spite of their guardian angel. We can pray to our guardian angels, but we have no guarantee that they will intervene. When we experience that a guardian angel has saved us from danger, God's grace is also always at work, and we have no influence on that.

At one time or another every adult has had the experience of coming close to suffering injury in a dangerous situation. Perhaps we began to pass a car on the highway and failed to see another car already in the lane next to us. Another accident averted, many people then spontaneously say, "My guardian angel was watching over me." Or when a driver approaching a traffic jam is just able to brake at the last minute, or when a car overturns and the driver is able to walk away without injury. These are times when we believe that a guardian angel protected us from harm. At such moments, not only devout Christians believe in guardian angels. Atheists may talk about their guardian angels as well. In these moments, we sense that we are protected by something that transcends human power. A guardian angel gives us the gift of trust that we will arrive unharmed again and again when we drive to work. The angel frees us from the fear of carrying out tasks that we need to perform but could also fail at.

The idea of the guardian angel is so widespread that it can be found in the soul of every person. Jews speak about it; Greeks call it *daimon* and Romans *genius*. Even when many do not believe in God today or find it hard to enter into a personal relationship with God, they still believe in guardian angels. This conviction is a kind of "searching belief" in God. Those who speak about guardian angels know that they come from God, and that God has placed an angel by their side. But in doing this they need not bear witness to all of Christian dogma. They are expressing an experience that they have had over and over again. This experience opens people to the dimension of angels. Angels are creations of God, and for us as created beings guardian angels reflect God's healing closeness in dangerous situations: whether we are driving a car, slip on the street, or are at home when a fire breaks out. The angel puts God in concrete form. Through the angel, the effect of God is felt in our everyday lives. Today there are many more people who recognize this godly intervention in their lives than can definitively call God their mother and father.

Jesus says guardian angels look upon the face of God. Each of us has a relationship with God through our angel. Every person is immediate to God. Our reach extends into the realm of God through our guardian angel. A person's vision is not limited to that which is visible and imaginable. Each person is surrounded by a mystery. We are not alone when we are lonely. We are not deserted when we walk through the forest by ourselves. This religious language, which is completely credible for many people in our postmodern time, would be thus interpreted from a psychological standpoint: the idea of the guardian angel brings people into contact with the protecting and preserving powers of their subconscious. These forces help people to take better care of themselves and to open themselves up to a life without fear. What is laboriously explained in psychology is clear to most people in their subconscious. People exist not only in the reality defined by their critical perception, but also in the "middle area," where they are aware of the connection between heaven and earth and visible and invisible reality. Because they have been intimate with this "middle area" since childhood, they have a natural feeling for the idea of the guardian angel. Without thinking about it critically, people express a heart-felt conviction that a guardian angel accompanies them and protects them from danger.

Helmut Hark, a Protestant minister and psychotherapist, often uses the image of the guardian angel in his therapy. In a therapeutic self-help group, he had the participants think about the meaning of the guardian angel for them personally. The following comments were made: "The guardian angel protects us along our way. It gives us support. It keeps evil away from us. It influences situations where we have been lucky. The angel causes things to come together. It intervenes in borderline situations. The angel sends me impulses to do good deeds. It is the twin brother of my soul. It is my personal patron. Through the angel, I am warned of danger. For me it is a form of higher intelligence. It speaks to me through my conscience. It's the spiritual proto- type of my soul. . . . It inspires my imaginative powers. Through it, healing energy is set into motion. It gives me an idea that saves the day" (Hark 141f.).

These comments show that today people who are unlikely to be familiar with the church sense that they are not abandoned. Through the idea of a guardian angel who accompanies them, warns them about hazards, and steps in to avert danger, they ex- press their faith in God's protection and help. They often have difficulties trying to imagine God, but in the angel God be- comes concrete. God reaches directly into their daily lives. The idea of a personal guardian angel in therapy often has a strength- ening and healing effect. Helmut Hark tells about a woman who was repeatedly driven by intense thoughts of suicide. In a dream she saw an angel "who conveyed to her a new — until then unknown — positive feeling about life" (Hark 143). Suddenly, her suicidal thoughts disappeared. Hark speaks about the spir- itual energy of the guardian angel, which often breaks through a self-destructive pattern of life to bring healing.

The belief in a personal guardian angel is more than a child- like idea of a cute angel who goes everywhere with us. If we believe in our guardian angel as adults, we will not only conquer our everyday fears on the road, at work, and toward threatening illnesses, but the guardian angel will also convey to us the feeling that we will come through personal crises. And those who are confronted with the history of their emotional injuries — for ex- ample, in therapy — and are left without a clue of how to break free of the entanglements of childhood will repeatedly experience the healing effect of their guardian angel. Understanding our injuries intellectually does not bring healing. Many people despair about themselves and the burdens of their past. The belief in a guardian angel allows us to have confidence that in the middle of the therapeutic process a kind of miracle will occur: a healing power rises from the depths of the soul, an angel appears to us in a dream and gives us a deeper insight, or suddenly the fear or the thought of suicide disappears, without our knowing why. The belief in a guardian angel frees us from becoming fixed on what has made us ill in the past. It also allows us to discover the healing energies inside us. The guardian angel who already proved to be our companion and protector in childhood is with us and in us now, healing and protecting our lives today.

2 The Angel Who Hears
the Cry of a Child

The first biblical story in which an angel plays a decisive role is the story of Hagar, the maid of Abraham. Because Sarah, the wife of Abraham, bore him no children, he goes to Hagar. And she conceives a child from him. Sarah becomes jealous and treats Hagar so harshly that she flees to the desert. The angel of the Lord finds her there and asks her, "Hagar, maid of Sarah, where have you come from and where are you going?" (Gen. 16:8). He then sends her back to Sarah. She should submit to the harsh treatment because it is God's plan that her son, Ishmael, have many descendants and be great. Hagar calls the place where the angel of God appears to her "El-Roi" ("You Are the God Who Looks after Me," Gen. 16:13).

Hagar finds herself in an archetypal situation. She feels like an outcast, totally abandoned by everyone. Abraham, the father of her baby, leaves her at the mercy of Sarah. She has no one who stands by her. The angel sees her and becomes her advocate. Although she has been abandoned by human beings, the angel sees her misery and does not leave her. Children often go through a similar experience. They feel misunderstood by their parents who scold them, and may even beat them, for trivial things. In spiritual counseling, adults tell me that as children they often felt as if they did not know what was happening around them. Everything they did was wrong. Their father's reactions were completely arbitrary. They always felt uncertain about what they should say or do. Anything could trigger their father's anger. Such children feel alone and at the mercy of erratic behavior.

The normal response would be to cut off all feelings and simply just to function. Fortunately, there are other ways of reacting. Children search for a place where they can lose themselves, where they can feel at home and simply be who they are. Such beneficial reactions could also be seen as the work of angels looking after children. Angels lead the children to places where they know they are protected, where the injurious and erratic behavior of parents does not reach it, where they cannot be hurt.

In these places children feel protected and whole. There, they come in contact with their inner resources and recognize — as Hagar does — the well from which they can drink. Hagar calls this well "Beer-Lahhai-Roi" (the "Well of the One Who Lives and Looks after Me") (Gen. 16:14). Many children experience church as this place of security. For others, it is the blanket they pull over their head that makes them feel safe, or they make a cave out of straw or blankets, or build a tree house, where they can withdraw from the outside world. In this place they experience the protection of the mother's lap. Other children speak to their stuffed toy, or pet their dog and tell it what is wrong. They know they are understood. Sometimes I am alarmed by the stories people tell me about their childhood. The belief that these people were not completely alone as children, that an angel was looking out for them speaking to them and leading them to an inner life-giving source, to a place where they could breathe a sigh of relief, gives me confidence that even people who have been deeply hurt can still find their way in life.

The angel in our story sends Hagar back again to Sarah. She should tolerate the harsh treatment because she is to fulfill a promise. Angels give such a message to abandoned and unfairly treated children as well. These children are also to fulfill a promise and know through their games about another world where they are important and creative and able to form a new identity for themselves. This is why they are always able to return home and withstand the difficulties there. For people who look at their childhood injuries in therapy or spiritual counseling, it is helpful to discover the tracks the angels have left in their lives. By telling everyone about their bad experiences, they often end up only feeling worse. Talking about such experiences can relieve the burden, but it sometimes also weighs us down. This is why I invite people I speak to to describe the places in their lives where they felt in harmony with themselves, where they felt protected, safe, and at home. By directing their view toward such "angel experiences and angel places," a new feeling of trust can grow. They recognize that in their childhood there was also an angel who saw their need and gave them the necessary strength to withstand the hardships around them. When adults come in contact with their angels again, they deal differently with their wounded past. We then recognize the promise to be fulfilled and the other world in which we were already immersed as a child, as well as the healing power that emanated from an angel and was stronger than the pain.

A young woman told me that as a child she had always yearned for the love of her mother. She had never experienced this love, at least not as she had hoped to. For a long time she pursued this love but was always disappointed. She became anorexic to "pay her mother back" for her lack of love. When

I asked her about the tracks of an angel in her life, she spontaneously told me that as a child she had often played games and in these games created her own world. She had assigned roles to her playmates and friends. The theme of her games frequently involved an inn or a restaurant. She herself often played the landlady. When she examined her feelings in this role it became clear to her what a healing role she had chosen. The landlady takes care of the needs of the guests, making them feel important. Everything is done so they will feel comfortable. The guests are welcome at the inn and should feel at home there.

The landlady was an angel for the child. She played the angel herself. Now, as an adult, she could try to come in contact with this angel again and take good care of herself instead of chasing after the love of her mother. The angel tracks in her life let her experience the love that she can give herself. Inside her is an angel who takes care of her. When she trusts this angel, she no longer needs to court her mother's affections. She has enough love inside herself. The landlady who prepares a cozy home where she always finds what she needs for life is inside her. She has the angel by her side who leads her to the "Well of the One Who Lives and Looks after Me" (Gen. 16:14).

The story of Hagar continues. After Hagar's baby is born, Sarah cannot bear to watch the child playing. She cannot stand to see his vitality and happiness. Unfortunately, it is still often the same today when parents cannot tolerate their child's liveliness. Instead of being happy about the child's vitality, the child is "banished," as Hagar was by Sarah. Parents turn their backs on their children and leave them alone in the desert of isolation, regimentation, disregard, and neglect. There they are threatened by starvation and thirst and wander aimlessly, totally confused.

For example, the hurt caused by the father whom the son loves so much leads to a jumble of emotions. The child does not know where he stands anymore. Because of his confusion he no longer has a chance in life. When Hagar runs out of water, she casts her son under a bush and sits at a distance from him. She says to herself: "Let me not look upon the death of the child" (Gen. 21:16). Then the angel of God calls to her, "What troubles you, Hagar? Fear not: for God has heard the voice of the lad where he is. Arise, lift up the lad and hold him fast with your hand; for I will make him a great nation" (Gen. 21:17–18). And the angel opens her eyes so that she sees the well nearby. "God was with the lad, and he grew up: he lived in the wilderness and became an expert with the bow" (Gen. 21:20).

Many mothers today experience situations similar to that of Hagar. They cannot bear to see it when the father turns his back on the child, when he is too weak to give the child support, or when he lives out his own needs through the child. Mothers cannot stand by and hear the cries of their children when they are starving or thirsting because they do not receive what they yearn for from the father. Hagar and Ishmael's story shows us that despite everything the child is not alone. An angel sees the child. The angel hears the cries of the child. It is comforting to know that the angel not only heard our loud and sometimes silent screams when we were children, but it hears us in just the same way now. Ishmael does not seem to have a chance. He is alone in the desert under a bush and is sure to perish in the burning heat. The angel who hears his cries shows his mother, Hagar, the well. In the place where we can only cry and search in vain for a way out, there is also a well nearby from which we can drink to fortify ourselves. Perhaps we do not see it. Then we need an angel who opens our eyes so that we do not become blinded by our own cries but are able to recognize the help that is at our disposal. This could be people who are nearby or a place where we can replenish our energy reserves, such as a cloister, a church, or a place of pilgrimage. It could be a special place in nature such as a meadow or a part of the forest where we feel protected. It can also be the well inside us, from which we have become separated. When we come into contact with this inner spring again our life blossoms.

We develop our capabilities, just as Ishmael discovered and lived out his ability as an archer. Ishmael becomes the father of a great nation. The possibilities that are inside of him unfold. He becomes an archer. The archer, skilled in the use of the bow and arrow, is a symbol of vitality and swiftness. The bow always connects two points with each other; it connects heaven with earth and God with humankind. It symbolizes our wholeness, binding opposites to each other to form a healthy tension that brings the arrow to the target. With this bow, we can become good archers, ones who hit the target, aim correctly, do not let life pass us by — ones who succeed in life. In Buddhism there is the image of the archer who shoots the arrow of the Self through the unknown to reach his true and highest being, thus becoming unified with it. The archer represents the spiritual person who desires to become one with God. Similarly the angel brings us from the middle of our desert into contact with our spiritual yearning, which leads us beyond the hopeless situation into a godly realm where we experience security, freedom, absolute love, and a place where we feel at home. Often we first realize what we are truly capable of in hopeless situations. It is then that we see our true selves revealed. However, we need the angel who hears our cry. We need people who are not afraid of our cry. And we need the inner angel who hears the cry of our soul and answers it.

When I counsel women who have been sexually abused I often ask myself, why didn't anyone hear their cries? The mother did not want to hear the cries of the child. In a weak attempt to express the inner need, she says the uncle had always been so nice to everyone. No one could ever imagine that he would do anything like that. Eventually the cries of the child became silent. The women buried their hurt inside themselves and carried on as usual. But they cut themselves off from life. They just wanted to survive and function so they would not have to face the pain. Eventually the cries break out again. An angel's touch prevents them from ignoring their own cries. They need to face their pain. But how can they find the courage to do this?

When someone accompanies them who is able to listen — without fear — to the terrible things that are revealed, they experience the angel who spoke to Hagar in the desert. They meet the angel in people who lead them to the well hidden inside them. But the angel can also be encountered in their own strength that suddenly arises inside them. In their heart the angel appears, revealing the source of the spring that flows inside them. From this spring they can draw strength to regenerate and grow beyond their old wounds. The angel promises them that in spite of all their injury they can grow to be a great nation and an archer; their life will succeed and they will reach the target of their yearnings. In therapy and spiritual counseling we cannot look only at our wounds. We cannot allow ourselves to remain fixed on our cries, as important as it is for the pain that is stored up inside us to be released. It is just as important to look for the angel who hears our cries and leads us to the well inside us. When we drink the fresh water from our inner well, our thirst will be quenched and our cries will become silent.

3   The Angel Who Opens Heaven

Jacob flees from his brother Esau. He is afraid that his brother will murder him. Esau is stronger than he is. While Jacob relies on his clever mind, Esau develops his physical prowess. Esau cannot forgive his brother for usurping his birthright and receiving the blessings of their father. Now Jacob is on the run. He decides to spend the night in the middle of the desert and uses a rock as a pillow. There he has a dream: "And he dreamed that there was a ladder set up on the earth, and the top of it reached to heaven: and behold, the angels of God were ascending and descending on it" (Gen. 28:12). God, who is standing at the top of the ladder, says to him, "Behold, I am with you and will keep you wherever you go, and will bring you back to this land; for I will not leave you until I have done that of which I have spoken to you" (Gen. 28:25). Here the angels create a connection between heaven and earth. They open heaven above the one on the run, for whom it seems to be overcast or blocked completely. Suddenly his life takes on great dimensions again. His horizon becomes wider. Jacob knows that his life will succeed, that God will be with him and fulfill his promise.

Often enough we find ourselves on the run. In the Bible there are many stories that deal with flight; this story, however, deals with a specific kind of escape. Jacob flees from his own shadow. Esau is the "dark brother," the shadow that Jacob has not recognized up to now. Flight is surely not a good way to deal with a shadow, because the shadow will always catch up with us. We cannot escape from it. Every psychologist tells us about the importance of integrating the shadow within ourselves into our own identity. If we fail to do this, an essential part of our soul is missing. But Jacob is not interested in such an integration and runs away. He must first go through a school of hard knocks until, after he wrestles with the dark man at night, he accepts his shadow and in it meets God. But first he flees, though not abandoned by God in his flight. Flight also has an important function. The angels, who appear to Jacob in his dream, open heaven to him in the middle of his flight. This has two meanings for me. The first is that we cannot integrate our shadow until a wider horizon is revealed to us, until an angel opens heaven above us. We need to have a goal before we can accept our shadow. When we are riveted on our shadow, we *have* to run away because our shadow frightens us. When we view our shadow in relation to the open heaven, it no longer seems so threatening. The open heaven also casts its light on the shadow.

The second meaning involves a recurring experience: just when our inner strength fails, an angel opens heaven, allowing our life to let God's rays in again. At times when we have run out of hope, an angel enters our life and helps us to see things in a different light. For many people a hopeless crisis becomes the moment when they discover their spiritual direction. The spiritual path is, however, not a cheap escape route or merely a detour around a crisis, but rather the only way that really leads any further. When nothing seems to work anymore on the outside, we can only continue along our inner path so that our life succeeds again. On the inner path we discover our true self, which shows us the way out of the dead end we have reached.

Angels also open heaven for children. For children from a

dysfunctional family, life often seems to be like living in a desert or in hell. We cannot live in hell forever. We can only tolerate it when from time to time an angel opens heaven to us. The angel reveals heaven to children in many ways. Children who are going through hell at home may be able to get great enjoyment out of a beautiful flower or find happiness when they lovingly pet the family cat or dog. Others can lose themselves in a game. At such times heaven opens above them. A different horizon appears in their lives. Other children get this feeling in the church service they like to attend. Songs are sung there that transport them to heaven. In this place their hearts are touched. A door opens and their souls become wide. Children do not reflect about how this happens. They spontaneously look for the places that connect their life with heaven, where a ladder to heaven is standing, on which angels ascend and descend. In these places they perceive that they are not alone and that God will accompany them and make sure their life succeeds.

The stone that Jacob uses as a pillow could represent the many obstacles that lie in our path and that we run up against and fall over. The angel transforms the "stumbling block" into a stone that supports the ladder connecting heaven and earth. In the places where we stumble, fall, and encounter failure, an angel can open heaven to us. Places where people have put a stone in our path can be those where our horizon widens and we are able to see our goal in life. It is not without reason that at the end of the story Jacob takes the stone, sets it upright, and anoints it with oil. It becomes for him a memorial to the place where God spoke to him and told him he would succeed on his path. Jacob pours oil on the hard stone. He treats the rocky and rough parts of his life in a gentle and tender way. In doing so a place of hardness becomes one of fertility; it is the place inside us where something can grow and mature. The stone becomes a symbol of God's blessings that flow over us just when everything inside us has turned to stone. We can often see in retrospect that many stumbling blocks became stones of blessings. At the moment, we fall we can only complain about the stone. But one day we realize that this stone caused something new to open within us and enabled us to begin a process of maturity. The story of Jacob shows us that an angel is also beside us when we stumble, and just when we fall on our face the angel opens heaven for us and God's blessings rain down on us.

4 The Angel Who Prevents Sacrifice

Abraham is put to the test by God. He is told to sacrifice his son Isaac as a burnt offering. Abraham sets off with Isaac, and they climb a mountain, where he binds his son and lays him on the altar. Just at the moment when he reaches out his hand to kill Isaac an angel of God calls him by name and says: "Do not lay your hand on the lad or do anything to him; for now I know that you fear God, seeing you have not withheld your son, your only son, from me" (Gen. 22:12).

This is a difficult story, which often arouses indignation in those who hear it. How can God demand from Abraham that he sacrifice his son? Does this not show us God's brutality? This story may be interpreted in various ways. One interpretation examines the story on a subjective level. Here it means that I cannot hold on to what I love most in life forever but have to let it go time after time. Only in this way will I be able to progress further along my inner path. I must not allow anything to become a false idol between God and myself, even the most precious thing that I sense inside me. My interpretation of the story of Abraham's sacrifice will focus exclusively on the angel.

It is valid to ask whether God actually demanded the sacrifice of Isaac. Perhaps Abraham had only *thought* that God wanted the death of his son. Perhaps his image of God was still incomplete. This is how the story has been interpreted by many exegetes, who feel it shows that human sacrifice was no longer possible in Israel at this time. The image of God had been transformed. For me this is not a story from the distant past. I often encounter parents who believe they are pleasing God when they "sacrifice" their children. Naturally, they do not sacrifice them as burnt offerings. But they sacrifice them on the altar of their own strictness and morality. It is the primary concern of such parents to fulfill God's will and abide by all of God's commandments. However, they fail to notice that it is not God's commandments they are keeping but the commandments of their own fears and narrow-mindedness. Because such parents are fixed only on their personal commandments, the children become the sacrificial victims. They experience only the coldness of the parents, who are fearfully focused on living according to God's will but who cannot sense the needs of their children. As a result the children are made to feel a deep fearfulness and guilt when they are caught playing games that have a sexual nature. A "fire and brimstone" lecture conveys to them the feeling that they are totally corrupt and sentenced to eternal damnation. In this way the children become victims.

It is not only a harsh perception of God that leads to the sacrifice of children. There are also many false idols that are more important for some parents than their own children. There is the idol of money or career. There is the idol of pleasure — those things we don't want to miss out on. When such idols have a determining influence on the life of parents, the children become sacrificial victims. Children are still tolerated, but their space is not respected. They are pushed aside so that personal aims can be pursued. Other parents place their children on the altar of their own ambition. The children have to make up for everything the parents have missed out on. They have to attend ballet class, learn to play a musical instrument, and at the same time take riding lessons. They receive tutoring in every subject so they can get good grades in order to study medicine. It does no good to reproach such parents. They need an angel to fall into their open arms to prevent them from sacrificing their children. The story of Abraham gives us hope that in situations where parents sacrifice their children an angel can intervene and bring them to their senses. This is an angel who makes them aware of what they are actually doing and opens their eyes so they can see what they should sacrifice. They need to sacrifice the ram that is caught by its horns in the thicket. The ram is considered a symbol of power. Instead of the helpless child, they should sacrifice a piece of their success, their ambition, their competitiveness, so that their child can live. When parents focus only on their own performance, the child gets shortchanged.

In this story, the angel protects the child by holding the father back. In this way the angel who accompanies the child teaches the parents. The child has something that breaks the vicious circle of the sacrificial ritual of the parents. The child, who seems to be helpless like Isaac and at the mercy of the will of the father, has an angel who repeatedly intervenes when the parents are fixed on their sacrificial ritual. If adults who were hurt as children look back on their childhood, they will often discover angels who held the parents back from harming them. An angel curbed the violent temper of the father. An angel intervened to lessen the beatings of the mother. They have stood up for the child time after time, despite harsh perceptions of God and honor paid to false idols, so that the child could continue to live.

Verena Kast describes people who have felt like victims their whole lives and persist in clinging to this role. They repress their aggressions, avoid conflicts, and have the feeling that they are powerless, at the mercy of other people's hostility. They remain passive and refuse to take their life in their own hands. They isolate themselves, fear change, and are stuck in their inability to act. "Nothing works anymore and nothing is allowed to work. Because of this, the role of victim becomes the most important one in life" (Kast 94).

The angel frees Isaac from the victim role. It loosens the ties that bind him to the sacrificial altar. The angel frees Abraham from his role as aggressor. By sacrificing the ram, Abraham sacrifices some of his own power. In this way Isaac can live. If children feel helpless, they are easily in danger of taking on the victim role. They then become apathetic and are satisfied with anything. However, these children are not really living. The story of Abraham's sacrifice gives us hope that an angel intervenes for children who outwardly appear to have little chance of breaking out of the victim role. Angels are by the children when they defend themselves against the aggression of their parents. Angels are by the children who have escaped from the shouting of an alcoholic father by running into the garden, where they find a safe refuge. There they are able to sing a song. In this way they free themselves from the threatening, arbitrary behavior of the father and come into contact with their own ability to find peace. Angels are by the children who are not satisfied with accepting the stifling atmosphere at home and join their friends, with whom they can express their liveliness. But what gives children or adults the strength to free themselves from the bounds of the victim role? Is it a spontaneous act? Is it a protective mechanism in the soul? Is it the child of God inside of us? Ultimately what gives us the strength to break out of the role of victim and to live our own lives cannot be explained. However, we can believe that it is a personal angel who watches over and prevents the sacrificial offering.

There are many people who persist in remaining in the victim role their entire lives. Living together with such people is not easy. Even when they take on the role of the sacrificial lamb outwardly and accept every burden that others have placed on them, such people radiate an attitude of repressed aggression. The sacrificial lamb conveys guilt feelings to others. Because the children cause the mother so many worries and expect so much from her, she does not feel well; that is the reason she is so tired and ill. Sacrificial lambs are a constant accusation toward the people around them: others are at fault when the sacrificial lamb collapses under the burden that others have piled on. It takes an angel to end this game and break out of the vicious circle of the victim role and hidden aggression. The angel falls into our arms and opens our eyes to see the ram. Instead of sacrificing ourselves, we should sacrifice the ram that God offers us. We should sacrifice some of the power inside us. With the sacrifice of our power and aggression life can emerge.

5 The Angel Who Blesses

Shortly before his death Jacob blesses his son Joseph and Joseph's sons, Ephraim and Manasseh. When he does this he says, "The angel who has redeemed me from all evil, bless the lads: and in them let my name be perpetuated" (Gen. 48:16). This is a beautiful image for me. All people have an angel who lays its hand on them and blesses them with goodness. In Latin and Greek blessing means "to say good" (*benedicere*) — to say good about another person. The angel who blesses is the same one who delivers us from every misfortune, who reverses misfortune and frees us from entanglements that make us ill.

There are children who rarely hear a good word. Instead, they are constantly being told that they need to do things differently, that they have done something wrong again, that they should finally clean up and stop being so difficult. Even worse are words that are more like a curse than a blessing: "You shouldn't be here at all. You will be the death of us. You'll see where that will get you. You'll never amount to anything. You're a burden to us. You'll always be sorry for what you've done to us. God should punish you for being so bad." I know people who felt like they were living under a curse their whole lives. They live with the curse that they are not worthy to receive the Eucharist and that they are not good enough to be fully integrated members of society, that they will never fulfill the expectations of their parents. Such a curse paralyzes the energy we need to live in the true sense of the word. Living under a curse means to constantly be in fear that it will one day become a reality.

The angel who blesses can be a fatherly or motherly person, a neighbor, a grandmother, a grandfather, a teacher, or a priest. It can also be the angel who speaks inside the child. We only need to hear the conversations children have with their stuffed animal. They often say words of blessing that, though addressed to their stuffed toy at the moment, are in reality meant for themselves. One time I observed a little girl speaking to her ball. She said a lot of good things to it, comforted it, praised it, told it about herself. This is the middle area that Winnicott describes, the place where the child learns the connection between outer and inner reality. In this middle area children use other words than those they hear from their parents. They express what their own heart needs and yearns for. The middle area is also the place where children have a sense of the angel who blesses them and says something good to them. The angel who blesses speaks in the children's own words. It holds its hand over the children so the curse spoken by the parents does not reach them.

Jacob calls the angel who blesses the boys the one "who redeemed me from all evil." The angel redeems the children from all misfortune. It loosens the ties that bind the children and cut them off from life. On the outside the children often have no chance in an atmosphere of disaster, strife, emotional chaos, and brutality. But the angel who accompanies them creates a healthy distance so that they do not allow themselves to be affected by everything. It loosens the tight restrictions of outer reality by bringing the children in contact with their inner reality, where disaster cannot gain entry. When the outer reality is too terrible the angel leads the children into the inner place where they are blessed, safe, and whole, where no one can hurt them. In this way, it is possible to understand how children often go through terrible experiences unscathed.

We should be on the lookout for the angel not only in our childhood. This angel accompanies us today in just the same way. It blesses us by giving us the promise of good, by giving the goodness inside of us a name. It loosens the knot that connects us to an ill-making environment and leads us into the inner place where the din of critical and hurtful people cannot force its way in, where no one can hurt us. In our inner place the angel of deliverance holds its protective hand over us so the disasters around us, which destroy and disable, cannot reach us. Nelly Sachs, the Jewish poet, talks about the blessed place that angels offer to us:

> Angels in primordial pastures,
> through how many miles of anguish
> must desire hasten
> to return to your place of blessing!

Nelly Sachs knows that we have distanced ourselves far away from our inner blessed place. Our desire must traverse many miles of anguish and let go of many things it has clung to before it can reach the inner place where we are blessed. These are the "primordial pastures," the first-created place where we encounter our own prototype and come in touch with the original image God has made of us. The angels protect the blessed place where God promises us his Word of goodness, lays his blessing hand on us, where we are surrounded by God's strength and grace.

6 The Angel Who Blocks the Way

In the Book of Numbers there is a grotesque story about the seer Balaam and his donkey. King Balak asks the prophet Balaam to bless his people and to curse his enemy, Israel, with the promise of a rich reward. Balaam sets off, though apparently without first getting direction from God. The angel of God places itself before him with hostile intentions. The donkey, which sees the angel with sword drawn blocking the way, makes a detour around it through a field. Balaam the famous prophet does not see the angel. In this respect the donkey seems smarter than Balaam. The angel of God blocks the way two more times. On one occasion the donkey presses Balaam's leg against a wall in an attempt to get by. On another occasion it lies down under Balaam. Each time the donkey is brutally beaten by its master. Then God opens the donkey's mouth and it speaks to Balaam: "What have I done to you that you have struck me these three times?" (Num. 22:28). Balaam does not seem surprised that his donkey now speaks to him. He enters into dialogue with it and makes accusations. Suddenly God opens Balaam's eyes and he sees "the angel of the Lord standing in the way, drawn sword in his hand" (Num. 22:13). The angel says to him: "Why have you struck your donkey these three times? Behold, I have come out to stand against you, because your way is perverse before me" (Num. 22:23).

This is not a cute and friendly angel but one who arouses fear — an angel who blocks the way. The great visionary Balaam is not able to see the angel, whereas it is recognized by his donkey. Reason does not recognize the angel who blocks our way to protect us from adversity. The donkey, the area of our instinct expressed in physical desires, is able to sense the angel who stops us on our way. Reason demands that we continue on the way we have been going. It tells us that we have to organize, plan, and achieve even more. However, our body puts on the brakes and goes on strike. When this happens, some people become angry and lash out at their body instead of asking themselves why it is being so difficult. God then has to open the mouth of our body so that it can be understood clearly. The language of the body does not allow itself to be ignored. The more we strike out at our body the more it will rebel, until we finally realize that our path is leading us downhill to our ruin. Then we are thankful that the angel of the Lord stood in our way so that we did not have to suffer even greater injury.

There are different ways that an angel can block our path. A doctor plans to change her job, but she is unable to find a place to live in the new location. Someone wants to take a trip but nothing goes according to plan. The travel agency loses the paperwork, and now it is too late to make another reservation. The boss of a company would like to push through a change in the company organization, but all of his attempts fail. Another person would like to become a teacher but every application for a position is rejected. Many people are angry when their plans do not work out. But perhaps we should first look for the angel who is standing in our way. Perhaps the angel wanted to warn us about continuing down this path. At least we should pause and think about the whole situation again. We should not be fixed, like Balaam, on the place we want to arrive at; we need to listen to the voice inside us in case the donkey is trying to bring our attention to the angel standing in our way.

In children, the angel of Balaam sometimes expresses itself through rebellion and refusal in particular situations. The parents think their children are just being stubborn or that they only want to get their own way. This can certainly be the case. However, sometimes children know exactly what they do not want. They sense instinctively the angel who stands in the way. They sense that a certain path is not the one that leads to their goal. Instead of lashing out at the donkey, like Balaam, the parents should pay careful attention to why the child does not go any further on this path. Perhaps the child is not able to articulate it. Yet, in the way children express their refusal, the parents can sense whether it is stubbornness or if an angel is obstructing the way. Perhaps the angel is speaking through the fear that protects children from entering into situations that they cannot cope with. When a child refuses to visit an uncle, most of the time there is a good reason for this. The child can sense that the uncle is not doing the right thing, that he is crossing over a barrier into the child's private sphere. These may be children who have been abused by their uncle and refuse to visit him again. Yet sometimes the parents do not let up, just like Balaam. They ignore the angel standing in their way. They do not want to risk a confrontation with the uncle and force the child to go back again. Eventually the child may give up and be abused for years. It would have been better if the parents had listened to the angel who stands in the way instead of being fixed on their own needs and wishes. If a child is being obstinate, then it is always right to look and listen to what is standing in the way. Maybe it is the child's angel.

The donkey sees the angel and understands it. Children often come into contact with their angel through the loving attention they give to animals. Many girls love horses. What fascinates them so much is not always clear. It seems to be the strength of the horse, which at the same time lets itself be controlled by a light touch. Girls can tell the horse everything that their parents do not want to hear. Children who grow up on a farm often love to visit the animals in the barn. After school they go to the barn first and tell the animals what happened to them in school and what is on their mind. Others pet their dog and have the feeling that it understands them. With their favorite animals, children sense something of the angel who is by them, protecting them with its strength, but who also listens to them and blocks their way when they stray into dangerous territory.

Balaam, the famous prophet, must be taught by his donkey. He cannot follow the path he is on any further. He first has to open his eyes to see the angel who stands in his way. The story teaches us that we cannot be fixed upon what we have set our minds on. We must keep our eyes open for the angels who stand in our way to prevent us from going further. Such an angel can appear in the protest of a spouse or of children. It can show itself in the refusal of colleagues to follow our instructions. Instead of using force to break this protest, it would be better for us to be attentive to whether or not an angel is standing in our way, one who wants to protect us from making the wrong decision or who is warning us not to continue on too quickly because the way we are going may be leading us downhill.

7 The Angel Who Sends Out a Call

In the book of Judges, God repeatedly calls on people to free Israel from its persecution by the Philistines and Midianites. When the harvest of the Israelites is destroyed every year and poverty is brought on the people by the Midianites, God sends his angel to Gideon: "And the angel of the Lord appeared to him and said to him, 'The Lord is with you, you mighty man of valor.' And Gideon said to him, 'Pray, sir if the Lord is with us, why then has all this befallen us?'" (Judg. 6:12f.). When the angel instructs him to free Israel from the hand of Midian, with the power God has given him, Gideon says, "Pray, Lord, how can I deliver Israel? Behold, my clan is the weakest in Manasseh, and I am the least in my family" (Judg. 6:15). However, the angel does not let up: "But I will be with you, and you shall smite the Midianites as one man" (Judg. 6:16). Gideon offers meat and bread to the angel, who touches the offerings with its staff. Suddenly, fire comes down from heaven and everything is consumed. The angel is no longer to be seen. Gideon then builds an altar and calls it "The Lord is peace" (Judg. 6:24).

The angel tells Gideon that God himself is by him. However, the reality that Gideon experiences reflects something very different. He finds only oppression around him. There is no sense of God's healing and helping presence. Many people cannot believe in God because they see no sign of God's help. They feel alone, downtrodden, exploited, hurt, and helpless. No one steps in to help them. The refugees from Kosovo and Rwanda cannot believe that the Lord is with them. They ask with Gideon, "Why did all of this happen to us?" The angel does not try to talk Gideon out of thinking that the situation is unbearable; instead he sends him forth and gives him a calling. He should stop the persecution himself. He should resolve the fatal situation. This seems to be unrealistic, and Gideon rightfully protests it. How does he, the youngest member of the weakest tribe, stand a chance of helping Israel? But the angel ignores this argument. It sends him out, confident that he can accomplish his mission. It addresses the power Gideon has received from God and also assures him of victory, because God himself is by him.

This angel story reminds us of the situation of children who experience violence and oppression and have no chance to defend themselves. They are robbed of the fruit of their harvest. When children succeed at something, they are not praised. On the contrary, everything that grows within them is taken away. The parents need it for themselves. They do not give the children credit when they are successful and have accomplished something, but use this to satisfy their own needs. They are not in touch with the children. When guests come these children are paraded in front of them as the "perfect child," and have to demonstrate what they are able to do. They have to recite a poem or sing something, whether they want to or not. The needs of the children are not taken into consideration. Only their "harvest" is of interest. Only their ability is important, as something the parents can show off in front of their guests. The angel does not protect these children from this kind of situation, but it does send them the call to take matters into their own hands and end the oppression. This sounds unrealistic. Children cannot completely change the family situation. But the angel gives them the courage to take the lead in caring for themselves. The angel is with them just at the moment they dare to free themselves from oppression. The angel reveals the children's invincibility that cannot be harmed by the oppressive power of their environment. The angel stands by the children's side so that they develop their own strategies of how to free themselves.

In counseling, adults have often told me about the strategies they used to relieve themselves of the excessive outside pressure they felt as children. One woman went to a field when she was a child and made a hollow out of hay where she withdrew from the world; a girl fled to church to seek comfort from Mary; another child hid in the attic, where he had a secret hideaway to play in. There each of them felt free in a place where the oppression could not reach them. A woman told me she found solace in the forest when things were not going well at home. This was a place of protection for her. There she believed in the angel who was with her. When we ask ourselves why children develop such liberating strategies, we can certainly explain it with the idea of the angel. Angels send children out, with the strength they possess, to do what is necessary to take care of themselves, to create a protective space that helps them to survive in a strained atmosphere. Angels send the children into battle, not into battle against their parents, which they would be sure to lose, but into a battle of liberation. There they find and expand niches that free them from the power of their parents. Instead of bemoaning the oppression, the children are sent by the angel into battle for themselves and their freedom.

When adults complain about feelings of helplessness, energy-sapping cliques at work, hurt caused by relatives and acquaintances, unfair criticism by their spouse, they should call on the help of the angel who sends out a call. In spite of all the oppression, they can find strength in themselves that is sufficient to free them from outside attacks. They have the angel on their side. They are not alone in their battle for liberation. The angel activates the power in us. It challenges us to look for strategies to free ourselves from the oppressive force of others. Instead of conducting ourselves like helpless victims, we need to get in touch with our aggression and fight for ourselves. Even when it seems on the outside that we have no chance, we can still accomplish something. The angel who sends us a call is fighting with us.

8 The Angel Who Gives Instruction

During the forty years that Israel lay under the yoke of the Philistines, God sent his angel to Manoah's wife, who had no children: "The angel of the Lord appeared to the woman and said to her, 'Behold, you are barren and have no children; but you shall conceive and bear a son. Therefore beware, and drink no wine or strong drink, and eat nothing unclean, for lo, you shall conceive and bear a son. No razor shall come upon his head, for the boy shall be a Nazirite to God from birth; and he shall begin to deliver Israel from the Philistines'" (Judg. 13:3–5).

The angel prophesies a birth. This is a theme that appears time and again in the Old and New Testaments. The annunciation of Jesus' birth in Luke 1 undoubtedly adopted elements of the angel manifestation in Judges 13. However, I will consider the angel who heralds a promise later in the meditation about the angel Gabriel. Here another aspect is important for me. The angel gives the wife of Manoah instructions about how she should take care of her son, Samson. The parents, rather than the child, are given instructions by an angel. By telling Samson's parents what they must do, the angel creates the necessary space the child needs to become a Nazirite. "Nazirite" means "he who is pure and holy, consecrated by God." This is a person who represents the original untainted image made by God of every child. Indeed, making God's pure image of us visible should be our goal in life, so that we become completely the person we are in the depth of our heart. All too often our life has forced us to develop a false sense of identity, pressing us into a mold that does not express our true self. The angel wants to lead us to the path of our true and original self.

In order that the identity of the child Samson is not distorted and his true self can live, his parents are required to adhere to certain conditions. The first is that the mother drink neither beer nor wine. She should not intoxicate herself. She needs to be sober so that she can recognize the mystery of the child. Many children are impeded in their development because their mother or father is an alcoholic. Then the parents are so busy with themselves that they are hardly conscious of the child.

A woman told me that her mother was an alcoholic. As a girl she could not even speak to her. The addiction made her mother unable to have relationships. She did not let anyone get close to her. Because of this, the daughter was never able to experience a sense of security or learn her own role as a woman through her mother. But it does not always have to be the intoxication caused by alcohol. Many people are intoxicated in other ways. They are clouded by their own illusions of themselves or their child. Their perspective is obscured, affected by hurt resulting from disappointment, resignation, fear, and depression. Then they are unable to perceive what makes the child special as an individual. In this kind of atmosphere, it is difficult for children to live out the original image of themselves.

The mother in our story is told not to cut the child's hair. Hair is a symbol for a person's strength. In some cultures long and flowing hair is considered a sign of freedom for men. As long as Samson's hair grows he cannot be overpowered by anyone, and so the angel instructs the parents not to rob the strength from their child. The razor represents everything that can cut the child off from his own energy. If the mother uses the child to satisfy her own needs she drains him and takes away his strength. If the father does not take the child seriously or makes him feel stupid, he will be unable to discover his own strengths. If the father immediately silences every aggressive remark his son makes with violent outbursts, he cuts him off from an important source of his energy for life. I counseled a man who developed a strategy of conformity and silence early on because of his violent father. This strategy had enabled him to carry on well for years. He was pleasant and easy to be around. But then, at one point, he had no more strength left and was plagued by depression. The razor of his father's violent temper had cut off his aggression, therefore robbing him of his own strength. He was no longer capable of defending himself against enemies, he could not assert himself in his profession, and had no will left to fight.

The name Samson means "son of the sun." If we think about it, every child is a child of the sun, a child in whom the beauty of the sun is reflected. Yet, often children grow up in a land of darkness where the light within is blotted out. In the Samson story, the angel instructs the parents in a conduct that allows the "sun child" to bring his own identity into being. The story seems to confirm the psychological view of children's extreme dependency on their upbringing. Perhaps we can also interpret it to mean that the angel who watches over each child gives the parents instructions to help the child. Often enough, something surfaces in children that shows the parents the right way to treat them. If parents are sensitive and listen to their children's angel, they can sense what is good for them, what makes them special, and the space they should give them, so that they can live out their true nature.

The instructions of the angel apply not only to the parents of a child but to every one of us. We should not rob ourselves by following some illusion we have made about ourselves. We should not allow a razor to cut us off from the source of our strength. I know many people who cut themselves off from the important life-giving energy of their aggression. In this way they become a pawn of other forces and allow their lives to be determined by other people. They are neither able to act dependently, nor can they say no to the requests of other people. They strive to fulfill all the demands placed on them. This results in self-inflicted aggression and hostility toward other people. This aggression is not dealt with productively. They are consumed by it when there is no clear aim of where to direct it.

Such people get angry at those who expect too much from them. They also get angry at themselves because of the way these expectations affect them. One woman was angry at her mother because she constantly insisted she visit her more frequently. I asked her why she was angry. The mother had the right to her expectations, but the woman also had the right to fulfill these demands or not. She was free to make her own decision. This woman needed the angel who gives instructions to better deal with her aggression. The angel would tell her that she should not cut herself off from her life-giving energy nor allow herself to become intoxicated with bitterness and dissatisfaction. She needs to see clearly what is demanded of her and what she can afford to do. With the angel at her side, the woman will succeed in life without becoming angry about everything around her. Perhaps some think this is a psychological theory and the angel is not necessary. The idea of the angel shows us that God sends messengers to concrete conflicts in our everyday life. In the place where we face our aggression, God's healing closeness shows us the way to deal with it soberly and appropriately, so that it serves life rather than consuming us.

9 The Angel Who Heals (Raphael)

An angel plays an important role in the story of Tobit. Tobit sends his son Tobias to a relative, Gabael, to pick up money he had left in his care. Tobias looks for a traveling companion and finds Raphael. Tobit bids them farewell with the wish that an angel will guide them on their way. He does not know that Raphael himself is an angel. The name Raphael means "God heals."

The story of Tobit describes two stories of healing. First Raphael heals Sara, the daughter of Raguel. Sara has been married to seven men, all of whom died on their wedding night. She seemed unable to have a loving relationship with a man. A demon loved her and killed all of her husbands. This demon symbolizes a complex Sara has about men. She seemed to want a husband more than anything but was incapable of having a loving relationship with a man and had to kill him when he got too close to her. Today such complexes are not as rare as one might think. If a woman is possessed by a "man-killing demon," no man will be able to remain with her for long without being destroyed.

Tobias is afraid to take Sara as his wife, as he could suffer the same fate, but Raphael encourages him to do so. Raphael tells him to burn a piece of the heart and liver from the fish they have caught along the way in a censer. The smell will drive the demon away. The heart and liver are the seat of the emotions; there is a reason that we speak about someone having a "broken heart." Love must be transformed in order for it to be healing. There is also a love that seeks to possess, a love that is deadly. Only when it is burned clean can it be transformed into true love. The demon who prevents the girl from marrying could symbolize her father, with whom she is so preoccupied that she cannot allow herself to get involved with any other man. It could also stand for her fear of sexuality, which becomes murderous when a man wishes to have sexual contact with her. Raphael heals the young woman by showing Tobias the way to become close to her. Through his healing he makes it possible for both to find happiness and true love.

Raphael intervenes a second time to bring healing. When he returns he cures Tobit of his blindness. He tells Tobias to spread the gall from the fish onto his father's eyes; although it will burn, "the remedy will make the white patches shrink and peel off. Your father will get his sight back and see the light of day" (Tobit 11:8). Gall is a symbol for aggression. In this story we can see how aggression causes a son to isolate himself from his father. Tobias must break free of this symbiosis; otherwise his father will remain blind. Only when Tobias is able to get in touch with his own feelings and achieve a healthy distance from his father can Tobit also experience inner healing. Tobias spreads the burning fish gall onto his father's eyes, and when he does so, Tobit is able to see his son as he really is.

Tobit's blindness is almost certainly related to his narrow expression of spirituality. He lives according to the law but fails to notice how his life loses its brightness because of the many rules he tries to follow with painstaking exactness. When laws become more important to me than life, I turn my aggression against myself. Tobit comes in contact with his own aggression in a positive way when his son spreads the burning gall onto his eyes. In this way his piety loses its aggression. Full of joy, the father embraces his son and says with tears in his eyes, "I can see you, my son, the light of my eyes.... Praise be to God, and praise to his great name and to all his holy angels. May his great name rest on us. Praised be all the angels forever and ever" (Tobit 11:14).

Here Raphael is not only the angel who heals wounds, such as Sara's possession and Tobit's blindness, but he is also the angel who makes healing relationships possible. He introduces young Tobias to the art of life and love. Through Raphael, Tobias learns to enter into a loving relationship with his wife, thereby eliminating the threat to his life. He learns to love his father without being controlled by him. Both forms of love are not easy to learn, because in both cases there are more complications than meet the eye. The love between a man and a woman can become a deadly power struggle, and the love of parents can hinder life when emotional ties are not severed. The Tobit story demonstrates how difficult it is to learn both kinds of love, and it also conveys to us the promise of an angel to accompany us and reveal to us the art of love.

Often parents have fears when their son brings home the girlfriend he wants to marry, and they are full of doubts about the man their daughter has chosen for herself. It is a comfort to know that there is an angel who accompanies the son and daughter and teaches them the art of love. Trust in the angel who accompanies their child along this difficult path relieves parents of their often excessive worry. The angel will enable a positive separation from the parents and make the love between the couple possible. At the same time, the parents are often proven right about their feelings: this man is indeed not good for their daughter, and the woman their son has chosen wraps him around her little finger and will eventually break him. Belief in the angel does not heal all the hurt that can be suffered in this area. Sometimes it is necessary for children to experience failure and to make wrong decisions in order to be capable of having a healthy relationship. When parents interfere too much in a partner choice, then their son or daughter becomes all the more set on whom they have chosen and even more resolute about standing by their decision, even if they have doubts in their own heart. However, because they do not want their parents to think they are immature, they suppress all their doubts in an attempt to prove that they themselves know what is right.

When a relationship breaks up, it is all the more necessary to have an angel who accompanies the son or daughter along their way, helping them to bypass detours and showing them the art of love. In the story of Raphael, the angel reveals his true identity only in the conclusion. Similarly, it is often friends who stand by the children's side and lead them along their way, even when everything seems hopeless at first. Sometimes the angel is also revealed in a premonition their son or daughter has. An unmistakable feeling about the partner surfaces, even when the son is initially blinded by his love or the daughter lets herself be used shamelessly by her partner. Everything the parents say against the relationship has no effect. They can only trust in the angel who affects the heart of their children, and following their lengthy journey, similar to Tobias's, gives them a love that succeeds.

Raphael also heals the relationship with the parents. Tobias has to first undertake a long and arduous journey, through unfamiliar territory, to enter into a new relationship with his father. Although he undertakes the journey on his father's orders, his father has no influence on him along the way. Here he is under the guidance of the angel. Raphael leads him into the mystery of sexuality and love and protects him from danger. And the angel accompanies him so that Tobias also knows that in strange places he is surrounded by the closeness of God. Tobias takes the risk of letting his father wait for a longer time than he had planned. When he sees him again he takes another chance with the burning fish gall. His relationship to his father has changed. He is no longer only obedient, but listens to the angel to hear his inner voice. And it shows him the way. When a son or daughter learns to listen to their angel and to follow it, the relationship with their parents becomes new, and they can interact with them as adults, full of happiness about the positive things they have received from them, but also with a healthy distance from whatever has made their parents blind and hard. Then they are no longer controlled by the voice of their parents, which has become fixed in their subconscious, but can hear the inner voice of their own heart. Here, their angel speaks to them and shows them the right thing to do.

10 The Angel Who Stills the Fire

In the Book of Daniel the story is told of the three men in the fiery furnace. Three young Jewish men refuse to worship the gold image that King Nebuchadnezzar has had erected. As a result they are bound and thrown into the fiery furnace. The raging flames kill all of the Chaldeans who are in the vicinity. "But the angel of the Lord went down into the furnace with Aazariah and his companions, drove the fiery flames out of the furnace, and made the inside of the furnace as though a dew-laden breeze were blowing through it. The fire in no way touched them or caused them pain or harm" (Dan. 3:26–27).

Fire has many different meanings. It cleanses and makes new. It can destroy. Out of fire one can also be born again on a higher plane. Such is the story told of the phoenix, the bird that burns itself in fire every five hundred years and then rises renewed from the ashes. For the church fathers it became a symbol for Christ, who conquers death through resurrection. Fire can also be a symbol for sexuality, passion, and love. Fire can be precious; the Germanic tribes never allowed their hearth fires to go out. Fire comes from heaven; Prometheus stole it from the gods to give to the people. Fire can also be an image for evil and the devil. It can destroy and rip everything down in its path. Fire has destroyed entire cities. The everlasting fire burns in hell and brings eternal torment to those who are damned. Thus, fire has come to be an image of torment and pain. Pain can burn like fire.

The king has the men thrown into the fiery furnace to burn them alive. Here fire is a threat to life. When the fire of passion burns inside a young person, when we experience the fire of our own sexuality, it can also be deadly. We can be burned in the fire of our own passion. Because we are unable to think clearly, our emotions can become like a burning fire. Young people often go through this experience during puberty and when they fall in love for the first time.

In this story from Daniel, fire is also a symbol for the king's hostile aggression: "[his] face was full of fury.... He commanded that they heat the furnace seven times more than it was usually heated" (Dan. 3:19). The young men are cast into the fire of hate, kindled by their refusal to submit to the king's wishes. For people who are obsessed with power, unrequited love or a refusal to admire and simultaneously pay them homage can result in this kind of burning hatred. The prophet Daniel tells us that the young people are not abandoned and left at the mercy of the fire of rage; rather an angel will enter the fiery furnace with them to still the heat of the flames.

Those who are victims of the hatred of others need the protection of an angel who blocks the fire of rage so that it cannot reach them. And people who are confronted by the fire of their own passions need a sensitive companion who stands by them — someone who is not afraid of this fire of passion and evolving sexuality. Like the angel, they also have to enter the furnace of passion. A good companion looks together with the young people at their passion without passing judgment. A good companion does not try to divert the flames by merely dictating rigid rules or threatening them with hellfire if the passion cannot be restrained. This person has understanding for the fire that burns, but also shows them ways to deal with it without getting burned.

The angel is not only revealed in the companion who stays at our side if we are caught in the fire of passion. Every person has an angel. There is something inside everyone that enters the blazing fire with them. There is something in us that protects us from the flames of the inner fire. We all have a place inside us from where we can observe the fire without getting burned by it. This place could be called our conscience, from where we are able to assess what is going on inside us. Or it is the inner self, the undistorted image of God inside us, that can perceive what is going on in our psyche without being determined by it. The story tells us it is the angel who is with us when we are thrown into the furnace of our emotions. It is the angel, too, who transforms the fire into a dew-laden breeze. In the middle of the fire is a place in us that is protected. It is the inner place of silence where the angel is by us, where God himself lives in us.

Not only young people undergo the experience of being thrown into the fire. Many adults go through such situations time and again. Even when they have encountered their sexuality long ago and believe they have integrated it into their identity, they are confronted by situations where the fire inside them breaks out again and threatens to burn them. An older man falls in love with a young woman. He does not recognize himself anymore. He knows no other way out but suicide. But an angel holds him back. It enters the fire and transforms it.

A woman who has been married a long time meets a young man. Although he is considered a freeloader and good-for-nothing by everyone, she is enraptured by him. She throws everything overboard and leaves her husband to be with the other man, who then only uses her. But the fire has such a strong control over her that she is no longer able to think clearly. Her husband and friends of the family can only look on, stunned and unable to understand what is happening. There seems to be no angel by her side. However, the hope remains that an angel is next to her and, in spite of everything, will eventually still the fire so she can see clearly again and be able to live her own life. The angel does not protect the three young men from being thrown into the furnace but only from being burned inside it. We can never allow ourselves to give up hope that an angel is standing by people in the middle of the fire of passion, fanning a dew-laden breeze their way so they will be able to free themselves from the destructive grip of the fire.

The furnace represents many situations in our lives. A house catches on fire and a brave fireman goes into the burning house to save a child or an old man. In a company, an employee gets caught in the crossfire of criticism. He is abandoned by many of his colleagues, but one stands in front of him so he is not burned by the fire. There are many conflicts between hate-filled groups that ignite a fire of catastrophic proportions, such as in the former Yugoslavia, Rwanda, or Burundi. We often only watch from the outside as people burn in the fire of hatred. But time and again there are angels who risk entering this fire in an attempt to calm the waves of emotion and to send a fresh breeze to the people through their love. And there are people who do not let themselves get caught up in the fire of hatred because an angel is inside them protecting them from the fire. The angel in their heart fills them with reconciliation and love, thereby creating a place in the middle of the fire that cannot be reached by the flames. In this place of forgiveness and compassion the fire loses its power, and it is slowly quenched by those who have remained pure of heart.

11 The Angel Who Frees from the Lions' Den

As in the story of the three young men in the fiery furnace, the king's officers accuse Daniel of breaking the law and praying to his god instead of the king. This time the Persian king, Darius, is friendly toward the Jew, Daniel, who has been abducted from his homeland. However, the other kings, the satraps, are jealous of Daniel, "but they could find no ground for complaint or any fault, because he was faithful, and no error or fault was found in him" (Dan. 6:4). Darius is torn between his friendship for Daniel and his duty to the law. He would like to save Daniel, but the satraps remind him of the uncompromising law of the Medes and Persians. Thus he gives in and allows Daniel to be thrown into the lions' den. In doing this, he expresses the wish to his friend that his god might save him from the lions. Darius, unable to sleep the whole night, hurries to the lions' den early in the morning and calls to Daniel. Daniel answers him: "My God sent his angel and shut the lions' mouths, and they have not hurt me, because I was found blameless before him; and also before you, O king, I have done no wrong" (Dan. 6:23).

The lion has always been considered the king of beasts. It is a symbol of power and justice and is often depicted next to the throne of gods and rulers. The lion can represent Christ, who is called the "Lion of Judah." But the lion can also symbolize the devil, who roams around like a roaring lion and looks for whom it can devour (cf. 1 Pet. 5:8). It is an image for sinful, threatening, and punishing powers. It represents untamed wildness and uncontrolled aggression. When Daniel has to spend the whole night with the lions in the pit, it can mean that he is at the mercy of his own aggression, his own savagery and murderous impulses. Aggression can be a positive energy that establishes a relation of distance and closeness. It gives us the courage to distance ourselves from other people and to defend ourselves against the injuries inflicted on us by others. But aggression can also surface in us and tear us apart completely. A woman told me that she sometimes sensed such intense hatred toward her husband, whose alcoholism made her life a living hell, that she would have liked nothing better than to kill him. She was frightened by her own unbridled aggression. Or again, something snapped in a man every time he saw a colleague who had slandered him to his boss and conspired against him at work. Aggression overcame him, threatening to tear him apart, and he was unable to fight it.

The aggression of children is often driven out of them forcibly. As a consequence, they repress their aggressive energy and conform in order to be good. But their aggression is then directed against themselves. They become depressed and weak. They need all their energy to keep their stored-up aggression in check. They lie on the floor and cry until they are blue in the face. Other children seem to be helpless victims of their aggression. The more the parents are paralyzed with fear, the more uncontrollable the aggression of the children becomes. The angel, who goes with the children down into the pit of aggression, is needed to protect them from their destructive rage. It takes the trust of the parents who, without fear, give their time and attention to the children's aggression so it can be transformed.

God sends an angel to Daniel in the lions' den and closes the mouths of the lions. When the angel holds its protective hand over us, we achieve a distance from our aggression. Our aggression is no longer a gaping mouth that tears into us and into our soul. The mouth is closed. There are monastic stories that tell tales of lions who have been tamed by monks. When people are able to deal with their aggression productively instead of letting it control them, animals sense this too and live in peace with them. This powerful energy is ready when we need it. Otherwise, it slumbers peacefully inside us, just like the lions in the pit with Daniel. Daniel is convinced that an angel of God closed the jaws of the lions. The angel, who conveys to us God's protective closeness, calms the aggression that seeks to devour us. Daniel can sleep peacefully the whole night next to the lions. As he gets to know them better, they are able to grow closer. However, he is able to do this only because he feels protected by an angel. The angel enables us to deal peacefully with aggression. We are no longer paralyzed by it, but can face it without fear and observe how it expresses itself.

The night that Daniel spends with the lions is an image that reflects our subconscious. Our subconscious determines whether we are devoured by our aggressive power or can deal with it peacefully. In our dreams we often encounter the lions who pursue us. They show us that we are on the run from our own aggression, which we have not yet learned to accept. In dreams we often experience ourselves out of control in regard to our aggression. We fight against hostile people and sometimes even kill them. In our subconscious are murderous tendencies, unbridled aggression, and animal-like power. But when our dreams confront us with the lion inside us, they do not abandon us with it. In dreams, the angel of God speaks to us. It descends into the lions' den with us to protect us from being torn apart. Dreams not only force us to examine the lions inside us. They also show us the way to become friends with them and how to integrate their power into our psyche. If we meditate on these "lion dreams" in our prayers to God, then we lose the fear of our untamed aggression. In prayer we can approach the lions and ask them what they are trying to tell us and what they want to show us. We might discover that they want to help us, that they are protecting us from hostile people who are trying to hurt us out of envy.

This is what Daniel discovers. When he is freed from the lions' den, his accusers are thrown into the pit, "and before they reached the bottom of the den the lions overpowered them and broke all their bones in pieces" (Dan. 6:25). The angel who surrounded Daniel, or was in his heart, protected him from the lions. The envious people who did not listen to their angel but were ruled by their aggression were torn apart by the lions. Later Daniel is treated well by King Darius. If we trust our angel, instead of fearfully staring at the paws of the lion, we will be able to go safely on our way under the protection of God. No matter how many people fight against us with their envy and jealousy, we will not be harmed. This is the comforting message of this biblical angel story.

12 The Angel Who Awakens Us with Its Touch

Elijah, a man full of fire and perhaps the greatest prophet of the Old Testament, is going through a crisis. In a mighty struggle, he triumphed over the priests of Baal, all of whom he executed. He seems to be at the pinnacle of his success. But now, Queen Jezebel is after his blood. Elijah, the warrior, is suddenly stricken with fear. He loses his will to go on and flees to the desert to save his life. There in the loneliness his own aggression catches up with him. He turns it against himself. He has fled to the desert to save his life but no longer has the will to live. He wants to die. He has had enough of fighting and cannot go on any longer. He had fought against the priests of Baal in the knowledge that he was fulfilling the will of God, but the motivation for his battle is gone. He has the feeling that his sacrifice for God was all for nothing. He sees no way out but death. He lies down under a broom tree and falls asleep. The thorny broom tree is a symbol for human sin that has to be cleared from his field full of thorns and thistles. By lying under the broom tree, Elijah admits that he is just as full of sin as the worshipers of Baal, whom he has fought against so zealously. He is dejected and disappointed with himself.

...and behold, an angel touched him, and said to him, "Arise and eat." And he looked and behold, there was at his head a cake baked on hot stones and a jar of water. And

he ate and drank, and lay down again. And the angel of
the Lord came a second time, and touched him, and said,
"Arise and eat, else the journey will be too great for you."
And he arose and drank, and went in the strength of that
food forty days and forty nights to Horeb the mount of
God. (1 Kings 19:5–8)

Elijah's whole concept of life has fallen apart. The ideal he had
created about himself has been destroyed. In this hopeless situation he is unable to go any further. He finds no path to follow.
He has lost his strength and aim in life. Every way out seems to
be closed to him. At the moment when he is unable to help himself any longer and his situation seems hopeless, an angel comes
to him and touches him. It awakens him and shows him the
water and the bread that has been baked in hot ashes. It reveals
to him a power that does not come from within. The bread, an
image for spiritual nourishment, gives strength along the way.
The bread, which has been baked in the ashes of his burned-out
hope, represents what truly provides nourishment when illusions have vanished. The water not only is thirst-quenching,
but contains the promise of life that will flow inside us again,
breaking our paralysis and filling our inner dryness with new
life. Water is an image for fertility and renewal. Bread and water
point to the transformation that takes place in Elijah, when an
angel touches him and awakens him from his hopelessness. It
is comforting to us that while Elijah understands the message
of the angel, he still lies down and goes back to sleep again. He
gladly accepts the refreshment, but only to flee to the realm of
sleep again. It does not seem enough that the angel only touches
him once.

Many people recognize themselves in Elijah under the broom tree. They are sick and tired of everything. They have no fight left in them. Eventually they reach their limit. They come to a dead end that they cannot find their way out of through their own power. The life they have built for themselves caves in. They had always wanted to create an ideal family life. Now it breaks apart. The children go their own way. Their spouse leaves them. Now they have no more strength left. They have devoted their time and energy to bringing life into their church community. Now their engagement is no longer required. They have become involved politically to create a more humane society. They have exhausted their energies professionally. Now they are left without support. Their ideas, actions, and strengths are no longer desired.

In such situations we need an angel who wakes us up. Sometimes it is a person who shakes us and opens our eyes, who gives us what we truly need to fortify ourselves. That person's attention, love, friendliness, and understanding nourish us. Such a person gives us what we need to go on. But sometimes shortly thereafter we make the same mistakes again. Then we lose hope and confidence in the help we have received. But an angel touches us again and raises us up. It opens our eyes to the resources that we already have in our lives that we can tap. And then we can set off on our way. It is, however, not a happy, lighthearted walk, but a path that leads us into the desert for forty days and forty nights. After forty days a new world appears after the Flood. After forty years Israel reaches the Promised Land, where it can fully live out its identity.

The angel who awakens us from our sleep of disillusionment could also be something that we have heard or read somewhere.

Maybe it is a passage we have often skimmed over, but now it suddenly catches our attention and shakes us out of our sleep. It can take the form of an inner sense of peace that suddenly surrounds us. And the angel can also be inside us. Through a dream it can show us possibilities that we have overlooked before. Or it lets an insight grow within us that enables us to get up again. Often we do not know where the angel comes from. All at once we feel ourselves nudged and awakened by its touch. Or it is a spiritual experience that comes to us out of the blue, during a meditation, or on a walk when we see a sunset. Suddenly everything becomes clear to us. We can get up and set off on our way.

If we look at our life, past and present, against the background of the Elijah story, we will discover time and again angels who have awakened us. The harder we fight for something, the worse the experience of the dead end we have reached. We cannot conquer all of the priests of Baal in us and around us with aggressive power. The more we fight against something, the more we are confronted by what we are up against. The thing we are fighting wants to be examined and integrated into our concept of life. When I entered the cloister thirty-five years ago I thought I could destroy all of the Baal priests within me with my discipline and willpower; I thought I could defeat my lack of self-control and stamp out all my faults and weaknesses. But then I fell on my face in just the same way as Elijah. My life became paralyzed. I sensed that I would never be able to accomplish what I had set out to do. In my helplessness I had to admit that I was not any better than the others — my Fathers, or my fellow cloister brothers, whom I was constantly criticizing.

Many people have vowed that they would do everything better than their parents. They wanted to raise their children better, to communicate better and more articulately with their spouse than they had seen their parents do. But one day they notice that they are no better than their parents; they repeat the same mistakes and hurt their children in the same way they were hurt as children. It takes an angel to free them from this vicious circle. And this angel is indeed present. We only need to take a close look and we will see the angel who has been next to us at every moment in our lives and who touches us and awakens us from the sleep of our illusions. The angel opens our eyes so we can see what nourishes us in our environment. Even in the desert, where everything seems to be barren and empty, there is bread and water, love and care. Here we also find the friendship and community of others who are like-minded. Even when we do not experience attention from others, we have a quality of love inside us that we are able to give ourselves. The angel in us points the way to the love that is already in us. It frees us from the constant complaints that nobody likes us. The angel cares about us and brings us into contact with the place where we like ourselves, where we can learn to love ourselves.

But the school of the angel is not finished for Elijah when he learns to stand up and set off on his way. After forty days he reaches the mountain of God, Horeb. There he goes into a cave to spend the night. The cave is an image for the lap of the mother. After wandering in the desert, he yearns for a feeling of maternal security. He wants to sense God as the lap of a mother. But God calls him out of the cave again. He has to confront God. He has to climb up the mountain where the wind blows in his face. There God shows him that he is different than Elijah had previously imagined him to be. God is not in the storm that breaks the rocks from the mountain. God does not clear all the obstacles out of the way and sweep us away on a wave of elation.

God is not in the earthquake. I would often like to experience God as a force that changes everything in me and around me, leaving no stone unturned and causing everything inside me to tremble and shake. I do not find God foremost in his power that destroys everything in opposition to it.

God is not in the fire. Fire burns away all imperfection and purifies. I do not find God in my own perfectionism, which attempts to erase all of my faults. I encounter God in the "quiet, gentle, murmur" (Martin Luther), in the "voice of drifting stillness" (Martin Buber), in the "voice of soft silence." God comes to me in a gentle way, softly and quietly. God is sensed as a soft stillness, as a gentle living breath. The angel, who introduces Elijah to this gentle and quiet experience of God, would also like to lead me to the God whom I can encounter foremost in silence. Every crisis I go through will also shake my image of God. I need an angel who accompanies me when my conception of God falls apart and who introduces me to the experience of the totally other God. This is the God I sense when I listen to the quiet and soft sounds of my heart, when I, like Elijah, go deep into myself and cover my face with a cloak. Shielded from outside distractions, I will then listen in the quiet to sense the God who approaches me only in silence.

13 The Angel Who Accompanies Us Everywhere

In Felix Mendelssohn-Bartholdy's oration *Elias,* angels often appear who speak to the prophet and comfort him. In his famous angel quartet, he sets the words of Psalm 91 to music in such a way that the angels, in this healing music, touch the heart and enter it: "For he commanded his angels above to protect you on all your paths. In their hands they shall bear you up, lest you dash your foot against a stone." On hearing these words we feel truly protected and borne up in the hands of angels. It is healing music, music that becomes a godly experience.

The words of Psalm 91 have always touched people. On our path through life we run up against many stones and wound ourselves on them. Lions, serpents, and dragons cross our path, and we encounter hostile aggression, poisoned atmosphere, and people who drain and devour us. The psalm describes archetypal situations. We often feel helpless in the face of the poisonous words of envious people. We cannot defend ourselves against people who make demands on us with their excessive expectations and who try to control us. The psalmist conveys to us the promise of the angel who enables us to step over lions, serpents, and dragons (Ps. 91:13). When we are in touch with the angel in us, lions and snakes cannot harm us. The angel brings us into contact with the invincible place inside us, the place of silence where God himself dwells. This is a place into which no lion can force its way nor any snake slide.

Two images describe the angel who shields us from the stumbling blocks, the lions and dragons. It protects us and it bears us in its hands. Protection means that the angel watches out for and over us when we are inattentive and careless. It means that the angel lays its mantle of care over us, covering us protectively. It surrounds us with its healing presence so that the hostile projectiles of aggressive people do not strike us, and the poison of their bitter emotions cannot hurt us. And the angel bears us in its hands. It carries us away from the earth so that we do not continually run up against the stones in our path. It carries us so that we no longer come into contact with the obstacles. It lifts us up to another level where we can see what is going on around us and the games people play with us. In the angel's hands we are on a higher level and are no longer affected by the friction in everyday life. We are freed from contact with the rocky and dusty road. We are liberated from the power of the vicious games that often victimize us and that we get caught up in all too easily.

However, we cannot allow ourselves to perceive the protective angel in an overly naive light. The angel cannot save us from the bad situations that completely overwhelm us and wound us deeply. It does not protect children from abuse. Yet, despite what happens, the injury does not have the last word. I believe in the angel who is by these children and covers them with a cloak of security that protects the depth of their hearts and bars the place where God lives from outside attacks. I believe in the angel who bears children in its hands so that they will not be bruised on the stones that people lay in their path and so that they can step over lions and serpents. In spite of the many injuries children suffer, there is something in them that allows them to cross over the poisonous serpents unharmed. For me this is the angel that bears us in its hands.

When adults look at their wounded childhood in therapy or spiritual counseling, they should not only fix their gaze on the lions, serpents, and dragons they have encountered repeatedly along the way. They also need to look for the angel who protected them, who kept an eye out for them, and watched over them so that they were not destroyed. When people discover the tracks of angels along their road of pain, they will sooner be able to overcome their past than if they only focus with fear and immobility on the lions and dragons. The angel is also by them now. Listening to the beautiful tenor part from the cantata by Johann Sebastian Bach for the Feast of St. Michael might also be helpful in coping with the past. The tenor sings:

> Stay, you angels, stay by me!
> Guide me on either side,
> that my footstep may not slide.
> But also teach me here,
> your majestic holy singing
> and the Almighty thanks bringing.
> Stay, you angels, stay by me.

14 The Angel Who Fights Our Battles (Michael)

In a vision the prophet Daniel sees a figure, in the form of a person, who strengthens him and gives him a message of comfort, "O man greatly beloved, fear not, peace be with you; be strong and of good courage" (Dan. 10:18). This figure, who tells him about his impending battle against the patron angel of Persia, is none other than the archangel Michael. Later in the vision Daniel is told, "At that time shall arise Michael, the great prince who has charge of your people" (Dan. 12:1). "Michael" means: "Who is like God?" My attitude toward God is determined by the archangel Michael. He shows me how not to put anything in the place of God, but to let God be God. Michael fights against the absolutism of earthly forces and the idolatry of money and power. I can truly live as a free person only when I put God in first place.

Michael has always been considered the angel who fights for us. He defeated the dragon. He is the brave warrior for God and is often depicted as an angel-knight, with helmet, shield, and flaming sword. He casts the demons into the depths of hell. Throughout the Bible, he is called by name only in Daniel, in the Letter of Jude, and in the Book of Revelation. In the Letter of Jude, a Jewish legend is told in which Michael fights the devil for possession of the body of Moses. The devil tries to claim the body because Moses killed the Egyptians. But Michael counters him and tears the body away, carrying it to heaven (Jude 9). In the Book of Revelation, Michael leads the angels in the battle against the dragon, whom he throws off the earth: "Now war arose in heaven, Michael and his angels fighting against the dragon; and the dragon and his angels fought, but they were defeated and there was no longer any place for them in heaven. And the great dragon was thrown down, that ancient serpent, who is called the Devil and Satan, the deceiver of the whole world" (Rev. 12:7–9). In many religions, the dragon is an image for forces hostile to God. Michael is the angel who fights in us against everything that wants to challenge God's position in our life. Michael is the angel who stands guard so that God and not Satan holds sway in the heaven of our soul and so that our heart is committed to God instead of being blinded by the world. Michael makes sure that God has power in us. Only when God reigns in us can we truly be whole people.

Cyril of Jerusalem said in a sermon, "As Christ wished to come to the people on earth, God the Father chose a mighty force, which was called Michael, and entrusted Christ to its care." Michael is not a sweet little angel, but one full of power. And God sends this power to all of us so that we will not be conquered by the forces of this world. This is a comforting message. An angel is beside us battling for us. The angel stands up for us when people fight against us, but also when we are embattled with ourselves. Above all, the angel fights for the helpless and weak and for children. Children in the period of the late Middle Ages understood this. At that time a great children's pilgrimage took place to Mont-Saint-Michel in Normandy. From Rhineland-Palatinate, Bavaria, Württemberg, and Switzerland children streamed to this holy mountain, where the archangel

Michael was venerated. They seemed to sense the need for the strong protection of this angel in order to live their lives in a world hostile to children.

Children seem powerless in the face of destructive forces. I get angry when adults tell me how unprotected they were against the erratic behavior of their violent-tempered father, how he might have beat them to death had their mother not stepped in. At the same time, I feel a deep sympathy for these people who were such helpless victims of the destructive force of their father or mother. When I reflect on it, I try to understand the father, who probably went through a difficult childhood himself and is unconsciously passing on his own injuries. He himself surely suffers because of them, but he is unable to behave differently. He is devoured by his past aggression, which continues to tear at him, overpowering the children. When I think about such children it helps me to believe that in spite of their helplessness and lack of protection they were nevertheless not completely at the mercy of the father; the angel Michael fought for them and gave them an inner strength to survive this battle. Sometimes I am amazed at how people can remain normal despite a brutal childhood, indeed, how they have accomplished great things. Michael intervened for them. He fought for them and even in difficult conflicts armed them with new strength. Through this strength they can now take on the battle of their own lives.

However, I often encounter people who have no strength left, who have been broken by the terrible injuries of their childhood. I can look at their wounds with them and talk about them repeatedly. Eventually the point is reached where it no longer helps to look at the wounds again. Merely telling them that things will somehow get better and that one day they will be able to take charge of their life is cold comfort. Here the image of Michael is helpful. They should place their trust in him. Then, despite their brokenness, they will sense not only their weakness, but also the power that lives inside them.

Most probably this has been the spirit of the veneration of Michael throughout time — people getting in touch with their own strength. When I direct to Michael those who have been hurt, they are able to distance themselves from their wounds. They look at the strength that God has placed by their side. When they imagine that the archangel Michael is fighting with them, they will not give up in spite of the futility they have experienced. Instead they will dare to take on a battle they had evaded before. With the archangel Michael they feel secure and protected in a special way. Michael shows us the power slumbering in our soul, which through trust in the angel will be called to awaken.

15 The Angel Who Heralds a Child (Gabriel)

Gabriel is the third angel mentioned by name in the Bible. His name means "God is my Strength" or "Hero of God." In the Gospel according to Luke, his primary task is to herald the child blessed by God. Gabriel promises Zechariah that his wife, Elizabeth, who is already advanced in years, will bear a son. He shall be given the name John, which means "God is gracious." And Gabriel is sent to Nazareth to a virgin whose name is Mary. "And he came to her and said, 'Hail, O favored one, the Lord is with you!... Do not be afraid, Mary, for you have found favor with God. And behold, you will conceive a son, and you shall call his name Jesus'" (Luke 1:28–31).

The angel Gabriel heralds the promise of a child in impossible situations, and with it a new beginning. Elizabeth, who could no longer expect to give birth to a child because of her age, and Mary, the virgin who has never been with a man, both become pregnant in a miraculous way. Men do not play a role in either birth. Zechariah does not speak during his wife's pregnancy; his view is not elicited. Joseph is not involved in the conception of Jesus. Pietro Bandini believes the announcement of the birth of Jesus by the angel Gabriel is a "statement on the narcissism of the male half of humanity" (Bandini 98). In the Old Testament God placed the man — Adam — in the forefront. "This time the feminine is placed in the forefront: Mary and her son Jesus, who, through his message of love, his exceptional regard for women, his rejection of the sword and all means of violence, has been proven the most 'female' of all prophets and religious leaders worldwide" (ibid.). Consequently, there is little wonder that it is mainly men "who should wage such relentless campaigns against the world of angels and the belief in angels" (ibid., 99). Thus Gabriel is also sometimes viewed as a female archangel, "as a kind of heavenly midwife for successful births" (ibid., 149).

The motif of an angel who announces the birth of a godly child is found in all religions. It is an archetypal image that also has meaning for us today. It shows us that the promise of an angel is connected with every birth, that every child is precious and great, a son or daughter of the Almighty with an important task in this world. An angel presides over the birth of every child. This is the view of the church fathers. Birth is not only a biological process but rather also always a mystery, a promise of something new, something that has never been here before. The two stories of the angel's promise in Luke 1 open our eyes to the mystery of our own birth. The angel Gabriel also presides over our birth. God sent him so that our parents could bear a child, so that through us something new shines out into the world, a new and unique image of God. We have a mission. We do not live just to exist. It is too little when we just survive. Against the background of the story of our birth, we should sense our mission in life. We need to come into contact with the angel who watched over our birth; then we will be able to perceive the mystery that we are. Rather then feeling worthless, we will discover the unique dignity that God has given each of us.

Birth does not mean only the birth at the beginning of life.

In our life we have to continually be born anew, so that our life remains vital. A crisis that destroys everything we have built up until that point can be a chance for new birth. The fire we have stumbled into can be a sign for the new self that wants to be born within us. Mystics loved the image of the birth of God in people. Spiritual direction is expressed by God's birth in us. When God is born in us we come in touch with our true and archetypal identity, and our life becomes intact and complete. In our times of crisis, hopelessness, and consuming fire, we need to be on the lookout for the angel Gabriel. We can enter into dialogue with him and ask him what he promises us. A promise is made to each of us. As much as we have to look at our past and deal with it, it is equally important to look ahead and to recognize the promise given to us. We have a mission. We have a future. We look at our past not to get caught in it, but to discover our calling and what has been promised to us.

Gabriel is not only the angel who makes a promise but also the one who interprets it. Thus Daniel hears a voice call out, "Gabriel, make this man understand the vision. So he came near where I stood; and when he came, I was frightened and fell upon my face. But he said to me, 'Understand, O son of man, that the vision is for the time of the end'" (Dan. 8:16–17). Gabriel interprets our visions. He lets us understand what we can detect in our hearts. It is not enough when the birth of a new beginning is promised to us. We also have to understand what God wants to set in motion within us. Only when we can interpret our life in the right way can it succeed. Only when we are able to understand what we see deep in our heart can we master our life. The angel Gabriel promises us the birth of the godly child within and lets us understand God's effect on us and in us.

Gabriel is the angel who plays a role in our birth as a kind of "heavenly midwife." Every birth brings pain. We must first go through the dark birth canal before we can experience the breadth and freedom of life. Gabriel is the feminine angel, probably the most erotic angel spoken about in the Bible. Painters have captured the erotic aura of Gabriel in many scenes of the Annunciation. Gabriel wants to bring us in touch with our soul. Helmut Hark understands the eroticism of angels as "their stimulating and exciting power in our soul" (Hark 49). Gabriel wants to make us fruitful, like Mary, so that our soul gives birth to the Word of God, so that God's Word becomes flesh in us. Gabriel stands for the erotic dimensions of spirituality. Living our spirituality also means the expression of our erotic identity: becoming totally immersed in the love of God so that it is reflected in body and soul.

16 The Angel Who Brings Joyous News

The most popular time for angels is Christmas. The Christmas angel decorates shop windows and homes. At Christmas everyone listens with fascination to the story of the birth of Jesus in which the angel plays such a decisive role:

> And in that region there were shepherds out in the field, keeping watch over their flock by night. And the angel said to them, "Be not afraid; for behold, I bring you good news of great joy which will come to all people; for to you is born this day in the city of David a Savior, who is Christ the Lord. And this will be a sign for you: you will find a babe wrapped in swaddling clothes and lying in a manger." And suddenly there was with the angel a multitude of the heavenly hosts praising God and saying, "Glory to God in the highest, and goodwill toward people on earth with whom he is pleased!" (Luke 2:8–14)

Children are especially fascinated by the Christmas angel, who appears to the shepherds in the field. Heaven opens for them and the cold and dark winter becomes bright and warm. Probably no other time of the year enchants children so much as the season of Christmas. At this time, they can feel that the world is not only cold. At Christmas they no longer sense the frozen feelings of their parents. Even cold hearts thaw out and become wide. At Christmas children encounter a love that comes from another world. This love is best exemplified for them in the angel. The angel is for them an image of pure love. It gives them a sense of a world that is intact. A shimmer of wholeness and peace enters a world that is shaken and wounded. The magic of Christmas lets them sense that they are safe and precious instead of merely being tolerated. No more do only hate and strife live in their house, but with the angel another world enters and suddenly their inhospitable house becomes a home.

Luke tells us about two kinds of angels in his story of Christmas. The first angel is the one who brings the shepherds the joyous news, to proclaim to the whole world, that the Savior, the Messiah, has been born. This is no doubt a fundamental conception of the angel. Through it joy comes into the world and transforms it. The night becomes bright for the shepherds from the light that radiates from the angel. The shepherds who are keeping watch over their flock by night remind us of our own sleepless nights, when we toss and turn in bed and cannot fall asleep because of worries, when fear and despair rob us of sleep. The sleepless night becomes bright. The Messiah and Savior responds to the uncertainty caused by our worries and delivers us from fear and desperation and heals our wounds. What happens during the shepherds' night watch can also often become a reality today, not only at Christmas but every day, when our night is transformed, when the darkness of our heart becomes light and we are relieved of our self-imposed vigil.

Adults tell me that as children they often lay awake night after night. They had doubts about the love of their parents. They did not know which direction to turn. Everything they did was wrong. They could never please their parents. They could not sleep because they were afraid their parents would fight again, that their father would hit their mother or they might be abandoned by them. They felt completely alone. When on such nights an angel enters and announces the joyous news that a Savior has been born, who heals us of our fear, then the child finds peace again and can sleep. The angel holds the vigil; the child no longer needs to keep watch anymore. In a story written in 1949, Ilse Aichinger describes how two sisters, seven and fifteen years old, yearn for the experience of the angel to overcome their hopeless feelings of being alone and misunderstood. This story reflects the author's personal memories of being a half-Jewish girl during the Third Reich. At that time Ilse Aichinger was truly abandoned. Her childhood was robbed from her. The only way to hold her ground in this night of brutality and persecution was through belief in an angel. "Better no world than one without angels," says the younger sister. But her world is destroyed. The life of the older sister, who wants to be an angel for her younger sister, ends in insanity and suicide. For many children belief in the angel who brings light into the darkness and finds joy in hopelessness is necessary for survival. They are able to tolerate their situation only because the angel brightens the darkness of their night. Only because the angel brings light into the darkness are they able to withstand the bleakness and hopelessness of daily life.

Besides the angel who heralds the Good News, a host of angels also appear in the Christmas story and praise God and proclaim peace on earth. They are often depicted as childlike angels happily playing musical instruments or singing together in joyful unison for the pleasure of God and humanity. Here something of the lightness of existence is revealed, embodied in the angels. Through the angels, everything becomes easier, lighter, and happier. We are able to sing again. Children often sing when they are alone, lonely in times of darkness, or when they feel abandoned by their parents. Singing is a kind of therapy for them. Then they come into contact with another world, a world of happiness and delight.

Many children are able to survive only when they sing their own songs against the shouting of their violent-tempered father and the constant criticism of their mother. Through their singing they separate themselves from the negative noise of their environment and sense a joy in their hearts that no one can take away from them. The therapeutic function of singing applies not only to children. It can also be healing for adults to let the childlike angel of joy into their hearts again and sing when they are taking a walk, cooking a meal, or soaking in the bathtub. A painter sang in our church choir. He often sang while he worked. Work was then no longer a burden but became a source of happiness. His own problems no longer got in the way; singing opened for him a way to life and joy.

According to Pietro Bandini, Christmas angels create a "conspiracy of love" (Bandini 105). Christmas angels join together heaven and earth, godliness and humankind, and the shepherds and the newborn baby Messiah. Like Gabriel, they also have an erotic aura. Artists have often depicted Christmas angels as erotic, childlike winged figures. Indeed, angels exist in the middle area between the godly and the human world. Similarly, the erotic is also a middle area between people, between man and woman. It is a current that flows between us. The angels of Christmas open heaven to us and give us the feeling that there is an exchange between the worlds of God and human beings, that here a current of love streams in both directions. This lends wings to our soul. The erotic aura of the Christmas angels affects our soul in a healing and life-giving way. The angel opens our soul to another world, to the world of godly love that breaks into our night and darkness. When two people fall in love, a new world opens for them. Christmas angels convey to us that a love, similar to that between two lovers, flows between us and God. If we open ourselves to this love, then our lives will be renewed, and we will also sense the magic of Christmas as adults. Despite all our disappointments, we will trust in the love that shines into our world with the angels of Christmas.

17 The Angel Who Appears in a Dream

Matthew tells us the story of the birth of Jesus from Joseph's perspective. An angel appears several times to Joseph in dreams. The angel defines the events for him. Joseph did not understand why his betrothed, Mary, was pregnant, and he wanted to leave her quietly. Then an angel intervenes in a dream and makes clear to him what has happened. The angel says to him: "Joseph, son of David, do not fear to take Mary your wife, for that which is conceived in her is of the Holy Spirit; she will bear a son, and you shall call his name Jesus, for he will save his people from their sins" (Matt. 1:20–21). Reason alone, even Joseph's inner enlightenment and sense of right and wrong, were not enough to explain the pregnancy of his betrothed. An angel had to come to his aid.

The angel always appears to Joseph in a dream. Later when the child is threatened by Herod, an angel comes another time to Joseph in a dream and tells him: "Rise, take the child and his mother, and flee to Egypt, and remain there until I tell you; for Herod is about to search for the child, to destroy him" (Matt. 2:13). After Herod's death an angel appears to him again in a dream and tells him to return home. Each time Joseph reacts immediately to the angel's call. He gets up and does what the angel tells him.

Today also the dream is the place where many people meet an

angel. It has always been a common belief that it is an angel who sends us a dream. An angel can warn us in a dream about danger. It can also define reality so that we understand it correctly. It can give us a promise and be a herald of good news. It lets us know when something new yearns to be born within us. The angel in our dream accompanies us along our inner and outer path. It tells us when we should set off for new shores and when it is time to return home. Sometimes the angel in a dream also shows us a whole new world, one resplendent with vitality and brilliance. Especially for people who live in a narrow environment and are controlled and oppressed by others, the angel of dreams opens a wide horizon, where the dreamer feels free and filled with creative energy. Dreams show us our inner treasure of which no one can rob us. Very often they reveal the beginning of healing to those who feel sick inside and have given up hope of ever finding their way out of the maze that is making them ill. In addition to the illness and neurotic problems inside us, there is also an angel who touches us and heals our wounds.

I often see the dreams people tell me about as angels who come to their aid so they are able to take control of their life. In dreams the angel transports us to another world where we feel at home, where we are respected, where we are free and in harmony with ourselves. Such dreams often bring about a deeper healing in us than talking about our problems. Deep inside we suddenly know the answer; we have found the way to can carry on further.

When I look at the dreams of children, it is clear that they are not only dreams of a colorful world that transport the children out of their own narrow environment. Children frequently dream about being attacked by snakes, bears, and dogs. Because of this, they are often afraid at night, immersed in a world of threatening creatures. It does no good to tell them that it is only a dream. It is necessary to enter into their dreams with them and answer the questions their dreams are asking. It helps some children to hold their stuffed toy in their arms when they fall asleep. They then have the feeling that the bear they are holding will protect them from all the hostile animals in their dream. In the same way, we can tell them that an angel accompanies them in their dreams to protect them from danger. The angel will wake them up in time to save them from being devoured. The angel will not let a single hair on their head be harmed. It helps some children to have a picture of an angel over their bed. When they look at it in the evening, they know that they are carried on the hands of the angel and protected.

Not only the night dreams of children are important, but also their daydreams. There they can create their own world where they are protected and loved, where they have adventures and are the center of attention. The ability to dream these dreams frees children from the raw conflicts of daily life. Then they sense not only the chaos between their parents, but also a world where a loving mother takes care of them and a father accompanies them on their adventures. These types of daydreams save the lives of many children. Naturally it can also be dangerous if children live too much in their own dreamworld and flee from reality. However, for a time it can be healing for children to get away from unbearable situations through daydreaming. In these daydreams, fairies and elves are present, and the existence of angels is just as self-evident as that of humans. They are trusted companions to whom one can speak. Sometimes they even carry children in the air so that they can see what's going on down below. In these daydreams, Herod cannot persecute them. His power does not reach them. The dreams announce to them the death of Herod. They can alway return to the real world from their daydreams without being afraid of what threatens them there.

Classic evening prayers are always prayers for good dreams: "Lord, please visit our home and drive all the snares of evil far from it. May the holy angels dwell here to keep us in your peace. Let your blessings never leave us." We pray that God may send his holy angels to us. They should give us an answer to our questions. They should give us a solution when we no longer know what to do. They should help us to make the right decisions. In dreams angels make us aware of dangers that threaten us. They also give us the remedy that we need. The angel in dreams is an important companion along our way. It warns us when we overlook something important in our life. It shows us the steps that we should take on our inner journey. It often gives us the gift of certainty that God is truly with us and intervenes in our lives. The angel in our dreams announces to us, as it did to Joseph, that we are godly children, and although persecuted by Herod — subject to the hostility of others — we are under the special protection of God. Furthermore, our life will succeed, even when it does not look that way on the outside. The dream is for many people the place where they meet their angel every night and receive direction for the next day. Happy are those who, like Joseph, get up and do as the angel has instructed them.

18 The Angel Who Serves Life

The angel enters our world not only in dreams. It is also with us in the middle of our desert, in our desolation and loneliness. This becomes clear in the scene of the temptation, described by Mark in two short verses in his gospel: "The Spirit immediately drove him out into the wilderness. And he was in the wilderness forty days, tempted by Satan; and he was with the wild beasts; and the angels ministered to him" (Mark 1:12–13). In the Gospel of Mark angels provide for Jesus during his whole time in the desert, while in Matthew they first appear after the temptation to serve Jesus (see Matt. 4:11). They transform the mountain of temptation into the mountain of paradise.

Jesus is in the desert. The Greek word *eremos* means "wasteland"—an uninhabited, lonely, deserted place. Jesus is tempted there by Satan. But Satan cannot defeat him. Even the wild animals can do him no harm. Jesus lives together with them, for angels are around him and serve him. The Greek word for this, *diakonein,* means to attend at the table and to serve with food. The angels nourish him and attend to his needs. They provide him with everything he needs for life. Satan represents God's debris. He tries to bring Jesus to the point of relying on his own importance instead of serving God.

Matthew and Luke have put the temptation of Jesus in concrete terms: being tempted with the desire to possess everything, being tempted with power, being tempted to use God to fill one's need to appear as a great guru and miracle worker. Jesus withstands this temptation. He remains in the service of God, open to God and obedient to God's will. In mythology, wild animals always stand for drives and desires, for the spheres of vitality and sexuality. Because Jesus integrates the areas of vitality and sexuality into his identity, he lives in peace with the wild animals. The angels are around him and serve him. The angels transform the desert into paradise. Jesus is the new Adam, formed in the image of God, to whom the earth is subjugated and who makes the unique and original image of God visible on earth.

For us as well the angels transform the desert into paradise and the wasteland into a home. They serve us where we are cut off from life, where our human identity is threatened by the traps that we wander into time and again or by feelings that tear us apart. They serve us so that life can bloom within us. There are children who often experience their environment as a desert, a wasteland where they perceive themselves as lonely, abandoned, and cut off from life. Everything is empty, gloomy, without meaning or connection. It just continues on this way. Children cannot live in such a desert for long and survive if angels do not come again and again to take care of them and serve them. Children then develop their possibilities in spite of the outer gloominess. Perhaps we ask ourselves where this liveliness, joy of life, spontaneity, and fantasy come from. It is from an angel who cares for them in the desert. And the angel who accompanies them also protects them from wild animals, from their own desires, which would otherwise be limitless, and from the uncontrolled aggression of adults. Children would be unable to protect themselves against the overwhelming aggression of adults if angels were not standing by their side.

Not only children experience such times of desolation. Everyone is caught up by life's temptations time and again. Satan sets the trap. It could be patterns of life from the past that we stumble into again and again. We fall into the old pattern of guilt and self-reproach. A priest I know always pressures himself to do everything perfectly. The smallest mistake recalls the old pattern of his childhood, when he was verbally abused and beaten as soon as he did something wrong. Every little mistake was generalized immediately. Everything about him was criticized, and he was called a good-for-nothing. Continually, the priest fell back into the old pattern that prevented him from really living. In these moments of temptation he needs the angel who serves life and protects him from the traps so that he can believe in the life inside him and in his own strengths and abilities. We will always be confronted with the wild animals inside us, with our desires and drives. They are unconquerable. We are able to live together with them peacefully only when the angels serve us. When the angels strengthen our self-identity, then we no longer fear the wild animals within. In fact, they will be transformed into forces that serve us and become signs of our vitality and power.

19 The Angel Who Rejoices with Me

In the Gospel according to Luke, Jesus tells us the parable of the woman with the lost coin:

> "What woman, having ten silver coins, if she loses one coin, does not light a lamp and sweep the house and seek diligently until she finds it? And when she has found it, she calls together her friends and neighbors, saying, 'Rejoice with me, for I have found the coin which I had lost.' Just so, I tell you, there is joy before the angels of God over one sinner who repents." (Luke 15:8–10)

Ten is the number of completeness. When the woman loses a coin, she has lost the relation to her center, and thus her balance. Now she lights the lamp of her consciousness and searches the house of her life for the coin. For the church fathers the coin is a symbol for the image of Christ we have inside us, for the true self, for our godly core. When the woman has found her original and genuine image of Christ again, she has a celebration of her own self-realization with friends and neighbors. Jesus compares the celebration we have when we have found our genuine identity with the joy that fills God's angels when a single sinner repents. In heaven the angels celebrate our incarnation. When we find the path to ourselves the angels rejoice because they want our life to succeed in the way intended by God. We all need angels in the house of our soul to rejoice with us when our life succeeds, and to give wing to our spirit and fill our hearts with joy.

The word "sinner" refers to persons who have missed their aim by living outside their personal truths; those who have by-passed God in their lives. If the direction of the path changes, if the right way that leads to God and life is found again, then the angels rejoice with us. The angels also help people who have lost their way to turn around and get back on the right track again. The Greek word *metanoein* means "to rethink" or "think differently." A turnaround begins in our mind. Our thoughts can often lead us astray. We often do not think in realistic terms, but create our own illusions of reality. We cling to ideas we do not want to give up or those forced on us by other people. We think what everyone else thinks. Our thoughts are controlled subconsciously by other people. We should learn to think for ourselves, to think in a way that fits reality. When we do this our angel rejoices.

But how can we learn to make this turnaround and to think as is fitting to reality? Our thinking is influenced from early childhood by parents and the people whom we most closely relate to as children, and it can just as often be distorted. We learn to see reality as others see it. Despite this, there are children who form their own opinions, think independently, and perceive reality in a different and genuine way. Children have an infallible ability to sense those people who are good for them. They avoid others whom they sense are overstepping their personal boundaries. They trust their spontaneous impression of the world and are often able to express it astonishingly well in words.

Who helps children, caught in the static thinking of the world, to express their own thoughts? We could say that children possess something genuine that cannot be warped easily by outside influences. We could also say that it is angels who bring children into contact with their true selves and teach them to think independently. The angels rejoice when children see reality as it senses it in their hearts. And in the same way the angels share children's happiness when they turn around after taking a detour or going the wrong way and find the path that leads to their true self.

At some time in life we all are diverted by paths that lead us no further — to dead ends that stop in front of a wall, to detours that never seem to end, to directions that lead nowhere. We have an experience similar to that of the prodigal son when we suddenly realize: things cannot go on this way, "I will arise and go to my father" (Luke 15:18). Here the Greek word *anastas* actually means "get up." This is the word that is used for resurrection. At some point when we are going the wrong way we want to get up and go our own way. Then we celebrate resurrection. Then the angel rejoices with us.

It was the angel who inspired us to get up, not to let ourselves continue drifting along on a way that does not lead any further, and to dare to defy everything that keeps us from the way to life. It is comforting to know that our angel also accompanies us along all of the wrong paths and detours we take. The angel seems to have a lot of patience with us. It does not leave us, no matter how far downhill our path takes us. We can have faith that it will express itself somewhere along the way and inspire us in our hearts to stand up and choose the path that leads us to greater joy in life, freedom, and love.

Sometimes we hear the voice of the angel in another person or in the quiet impulses of our heart, but only first when we, like the woman in the parable, have first lost a coin and lost our balance. But it is never too late to stand up and light the flame of our consciousness, to set off on the search for our lost identity, and to celebrate the festival of our becoming whole, of becoming one with God. Then the angel celebrates and rejoices with us.

20 The Angel Who Takes Away Fear

In the scene on the Mount of Olives in Luke, an angel appears to Jesus as he struggles in prayer and strengthens him. Jesus is afraid. He is faced with the question of whether he should run away or remain steadfast. He struggles with God over whether or not it could be God's will that he has to die. He wanted to bring people the message of the compassionate Father. He wanted to prove to them the goodness and benevolence of God toward humankind, and lead them to the path of peace and life. But then the Sadducees, the Jewish representatives hostile to Rome, turned against him. Should he be unfaithful to his mission and only save himself? Could it be that God would allow him to suffer a violent death? In his struggle Jesus fervently prays, " 'Father, if it is your will, take this cup away from me; nevertheless not my will, but yours, be done.' Then an angel of the Lord appeared to him from heaven, strengthening him" (Luke 22:42f).

The angel stands by him when he is afraid. Luke describes the fear of Jesus very realistically: "And being in agony, he prayed more earnestly. Then his sweat became like great drops of blood falling down to the ground" (Luke 22:44). The Greek word for fear here is *agonia.* It comes from *agon,* meaning fight, competition. *Agonia* is the inner turmoil, the worry, the fear of an uncertain victory, "the final tensing of forces before impending decisions and catastrophes" (Stauffer, *Theologisches Wörterbuch* 1:140). This is mortal agony, a last gathering of all inner forces in the final moment of life before one is to be killed. For Jesus it is the fear of falling into nothingness, the fear of the fight between life and death, the fear of a torment that he cannot gauge, the fear of the capriciousness of a power to which he is helplessly subjected. In this fear, the angel stands by Jesus; it strengthens him and transforms the fear. After this struggle Jesus goes to the apostles, composed and upright, and says to them: "Why do you sleep? Rise and pray lest you enter into temptation" (Luke 22:46). Prayer helped Jesus to find clarity in the temptation and confusion and to gain strength for his way.

Many people today are visited by fear. Even when they do not show their fear on the surface, it is their constant companion. If they are able to speak openly about themselves, it is their central topic. There is the fear of failure, the fear of humiliation, the fear of looking foolish in front of other people. Others have a fear of people who wield power. They panic when others criticize them and confront them with their authority. It is the fear that these people can do what they want with them. It may also be the fear of being rejected by others, no longer being loved because of a mistake one has made. Or it is a diffuse fear that cannot be pinpointed exactly. It can be a fear of the dark, a fear of close spaces, of hospitals or burglars. We can suffer existential fears of disease and death, the fear of not accomplishing enough or of life passing us by. Our fears are bred by primal fears that seem to be a part of our makeup as humans. These are fears located in our collective subconscious, those that are addressed by people of all nations in their sagas and myths: the fear of annihilation, of being consumed and destroyed.

Fear that surfaces in concrete situations is increased by childhood experiences that elicited fear. A woman was forced to stay for a long time in the hospital when she was a child and never received a visit from anyone. Fear still takes hold of her when she goes to a hospital to visit a patient. In some situations she has a fear of loss, which shows itself to be completely unjustified in light of the outer circumstances. She is aware of these primal fears and in the meantime has also become better able to deal with them; however, they still surface and increase her fear triggered by concrete situations. Another woman has a fear of every kind of authority. She is then immediately reminded of her father who brutally beat her and against whom she was powerless and unable to protect herself. Anytime she is spoken to loudly, the primal childhood fear of the screaming and violent father resurfaces.

There are fears that can be brought to light and worked out in therapy, but not completely erased. They remain in spite of all the conscious attempts made to come to terms with them. We can try to live with them. When the roots of fear are known we no longer condemn ourselves when it surfaces. We accept it and are therefore able to see it in a relative manner. It does no good to fight against fear because this only makes it stronger. I have to come to terms with my fears and allow myself to accept what I am afraid of. For example, I can imagine that I humiliate myself, that I begin to stutter or start to sweat because of nervousness and uncertainty. What happens then? Are the consequences really as bad as I imagine? Does everyone really reject me? Or is it I myself who cannot forgive myself when I make a mistake? I can also imagine that an angel accompanies me when I am afraid, that I am not alone with my fear. The fear is allowed to exist, but in my fear I am aware of the angel who is by me. The angel inside me brings me into contact with the trust that is always in me next to my fear. Jesus' fear did not vanish at once when the angel gave him strength. But something had been transformed for him. If I imagine that an angel is by me when I am afraid, my fear does not disappear; however, a spark of hope enters it. Sometimes fear seems like a bottomless pit. We have the sensation of losing our footing. The idea that my angel is also beside me in this abyss gives me a piece of ground under my feet, even if it's not entirely solid.

I am not completely at the mercy of fear; with the angel at my side I am also able to experience a place of trust.

21 *The Angel Who Breaks the Chains*

In the Acts of the Apostles, Luke tells us how Peter is miraculously freed from prison by an angel. Herod had ordered Peter to be thrown into prison:

> The very night when Herod was about to bring him out, Peter was sleeping between two soldiers, bound with two chains, and sentries before the door were guarding the prison; and behold an angel of the Lord appeared, and a light shone in the cell; and he struck Peter on the side and woke him, saying, "Get up quickly." And the chains fell off his hands. And the angel said to him, "Gird yourself and tie on your sandals." And he did so. And he said to him, "Wrap your mantle around you and follow me." And he went out and followed him; he did not know that what was done by the angel was real, but thought he was seeing a vision. When they had passed the first and second guard, they came to the iron gate leading into the city. It opened to them of its own accord, and they went out and passed on through one street; and immediately the angel left him." (Acts 12:6–10)

Many people feel like Peter in the prison, bound and guarded by two soldiers. Peter has no chance. The prison can be the fear that keeps us chained. It can also be a relationship in which we feel like a prisoner. Prison can be the limitations we set on ourselves, when we have the feeling we cannot escape from ourselves: tangled up in our emotions, captured by our passions, and full of inhibitions and blockades. Soldiers are on the left and right of us. They represent the law. Often our inner prison is guarded by those who represent authority and by our own superego, which drives us on making us think we should do one thing instead of another and causing us to find fault within ourselves. The soldiers punish us immediately when we have acted against the voice of the superego. They treat us brutally. Peter is even forced to sleep between these two soldiers. He has no room to move. The superego can become a controlling force that follows us everywhere, even in our sleep. It judges and condemns everything we do. When we are happy because we have succeeded at something, an inner judgment immediately follows that we are being proud. If we want to say something, we are put under pressure by the superego to make everything sound right.

Many people feel they have as little chance in their prison as Peter. They also need an angel to come to them in the middle of the night and free them from their chains, to nudge them to get up and set off on the way that leads to freedom. Getting up is something the prisoner has to do alone. Only when we take action ourselves can the chains fall from our hands. The angel gives additional orders: "Gird yourself and tie on your sandals. . . . Wrap your mantle around you and follow me" (Acts 12:8). Those who feel imprisoned in their passions and drives, in fears and depression, have to gird themselves with their own power. This is an image not only for our own strength, but also for the readiness to set off on the way and to follow the angel. As long as the angel leads the way, the guards do not attack. The guards of the ego are powerless in the face of the angel. When we come into contact with the angel, the voice of the ego is silenced. The angel opens the door and leads us into freedom, into life, into the city.

Perhaps the angel also comes to us while we are sleeping in a dream. Peter can hardly differentiate whether what is happening is a dream or reality. The dream becomes reality. He has indeed escaped from prison. When the angel comes to us, we also often do not know whether it is a dream or reality. However, the dream is also a truth that has an effect on our outer reality. When the bonds are loosened in a dream, then we will be able to enter the reality of everyday life as freer individuals. What happens in the subconscious is real and has an effect that goes deep into conscious reality. If I dream about my prison walls falling down, then in reality my prison also has been unlocked. When I dream that my persecutor has lost sight of me, then I am already a step further on the way to claiming my self-identity.

22 The Angel Who Enables Resurrection

Angels play an important role in all the gospel accounts of the resurrection. They witness the resurrection and reveal to the women and disciples the mystery of the empty tomb.

In the Gospel of Matthew, the angel of the Lord not only testifies to the resurrection, but also seems to bring it about and to accompany it.

Now after the Sabbath, as the first day of the week began to dawn, Mary Magdalene and the other Mary came to see the tomb. And behold, there was a great earthquake; for an angel of the Lord descended from heaven, and came and rolled back the stone from the door, and sat on it. His countenance was like lightning, and his clothing as white as snow. And the guards shook for fear of him, and became like dead men. But the angel answered and said to the women, "Do not be afraid, for I know that you seek Jesus who was crucified. He is not here; for he is risen, as he said. Come, see the place where the Lord lay. And go quickly and tell his disciples that he is risen from the dead, and indeed he is going before you into Galilee; there you will see him. Behold, I have told you." So they went out quickly from the tomb with fear and great joy, and ran to bring his disciples word. (Matt. 28:1–8)

In the Gospel of Matthew, the women do not come to the tomb to anoint the body of Jesus but to see the tomb. Here the Greek word *theorein* is used. This means: "to view," "to meditate," "to look at." They arrive in the late evening because the new day begins after twilight. They want to remain the whole night at the tomb, to mourn Jesus, to think about him, and to meditate. A great earthquake occurs. Everything is shaken and movement comes into the frozen moment of silence at the tomb. The angel of the Lord descends from heaven. Earthquakes and the appearance of angels are the two most important characteristics of encounters with God in the Old Testament. When God appears and intervenes in the world, his appearance is signaled by angels and earthquakes.

The angel rolls the stone away from the tomb and sits down on it. A stone often presses down on us, blocking us and keeping us from living. It lies on the precise place where life wants to blossom out. Under the stone life is stifled from unfolding. The angel knows what is blocking us and loosens the stone where it most hinders us from living. And then the angel sits down on the stone. It transforms the stone, which blocks us, into a stone that shows us God's liberating presence.

The angel in this story is full of power. It shines like a flash of lightning in the darkness. The sentries standing guard tremble with fear. They are like dead men, while the one they are guarding has risen to life. There are such sentries who guard what is dead inside us, who guard lest something within us dares to change, so that things stay the same and our principles are not shaken. When the angel breaks into our tomb-like world, the sentries fall to the ground. They can no longer prevent the life in us from blossoming out and unfolding.

A mighty power radiates from this angel who bursts open the tomb that we have made for ourselves out of resignation and disappointment. The angel does not let us sleep peacefully in our tomb. It shakes us awake. Resurrection is not just something from the past. The angel of the Lord wants to effect a resurrection in us as well, by rolling away the stone that blocks us. Many of us would rather stay confined in our tombs. Although we complain about how damp and dark it is inside, we are afraid to get out, because if we did we would have to confront life. Then we could be wounded. Then we would no longer have an excuse for the refusal into which we have settled. Then it takes an angel to shake us and set something inside us in motion and force us out of our graves.

The angel causes consternation and fear but tells the women not to be afraid. It shows them that the grave is empty and that Jesus has risen from the dead. They will no longer find him in the grave or in the past. Jesus is no longer to be mourned in what has been. He has preceded the women to Galilee. They will find him in Galilee, not in the holy city of Jerusalem, but in the scorned place of Galilee, where Jews and pagans live in a mixed community. We will see and encounter the Resurrected One in the place where we live, where the pious mix with the pagan, god-closeness with god-distance, the familiar with the unknown, in the place where we dislike ourselves. In the middle of the confusion of the world we will experience resurrection. In the middle of our self-contempt the Resurrected One will lift us up.

The angel sends the women forth so they will become angels of the resurrection themselves and announce the Good News of Jesus' resurrection from the dead to the disciples. Initially the women had only come to see the grave. They wanted to remain spectators. Now they receive a mission. They should go forth to the disciples and testify to them that life has triumphed over death, that love is stronger than hate, that the stone that shuts off life has been rolled away and the tomb opened up. The women leave the grave joyfully, but at the same time fearfully. They are moved by all that has taken place. The angel not only was for them a witness of Jesus' resurrection, but also brought about their own personal resurrection. They have risen and set off on their way. On this path they meet the Resurrected One himself. They then know the truth of the angel's message, and thus become angels — messengers of the resurrection — for others.

This is probably the greatest effect that an angel can have on our lives: it can roll away the stone and enable us to get up out of the grave. It is so much easier to remain where we are and to pass the responsibility for ourselves on to others instead of getting up through our own power. It is more comfortable to feel like a victim than to take responsibility for ourselves. The angel who accompanies us hinders us from remaining in the victim role. It moves the stone from our tomb so that we can get up alone and confront life. The angel brings us in contact with our own strength. It is not only outside but also inside. Sometimes we need people as angels to roll away the stone and give us the courage to stand up. However, getting up is something we have to do for ourselves. That means trusting the strength the angel awakens in us, the strength we have in ourselves.

The knowledge of the grave is given to us as children. When we were children we might have ceremoniously buried a dead bird and placed a cross on its grave. It seemed we could sense that everything dead has to be buried. Only in this way can it be transformed and resurrected. We have to bury the old, whatever has become a thing of the past, instead of dragging it around with us for a lifetime. Some children experience the grave in a different way. They feel like they are in a grave, pressed under a tombstone. They are unable to come to life. Everything that takes place seems to happen in a fog. The oppressive atmosphere in the family home covers everything that wants to blossom out with vitality. It is like a stone that lies on top of them and keeps them from living. Sometimes children seem to be unresponsive. They live in another world; the great stone makes reality unapproachable for them. Parents are often anxious when their children withdraw into this tomb. They do not know if an angel will descend to the grave in the middle of the night and move the stone away. The story of the resurrection in Matthew wants to awaken our trust that the state of the grave does not remain permanent for children or adults. When everything is dark and full of sadness and life is covered in depression, an angel comes down from heaven and causes an earthquake. When the angel, in the form of a faithful friend, a dream, or an inner experience, descends into our grave-like situation, we will be able to get up and live. The angel can come to us like a flash of lightning, a flash of inspiration that brightens our darkness and creates the place for resurrection.

23 The Angel Who Interprets Our Life

In the Gospel of Luke, the angels have another meaning for the resurrection. They interpret the resurrection event for the women. The women enter the tomb to find the body of Jesus gone. They do not understand what this means:

> And it happened, as they were greatly perplexed about this, that behold two men stood by them in shining garments. Then, as they were afraid and bowed their faces to the earth, they said to them, "Why do you seek the living among the dead? He is not here, but is risen! Remember how he spoke to you when he was in still in Galilee, saying: The Son of Man must be delivered into the hands of sinful men, and be crucified, and on the third day rise again." And they remembered his words. Then they returned from the tomb and told all these things to the eleven and to all the rest. (Luke 24:2–9)

As in the Old Testament the angels here are described as men. Their shining robes signify that they are angels. The question of the two angels, "Why do you seek the living among the dead?" is in the form of an aphorism. They should not look for the One who is resurrected in the tomb — the realm of the dead. This aphorism also has relevance for us today. Many pious people look for Jesus in the realm of the dead, in words that have lost their meaning and in an empty piety made up of rules. Others look for Jesus only in the past. They focus only on traditional forms instead of confronting their lives. Some use their spiritual direction to evade life instead of opening themselves up so life can enter. Others look for life in dead things when they search for happiness in money, possessions, power, career, or prestige. But resurrection means to discover the life within ourselves and to cease trying to find it in dead things.

The two angels interpret the resurrection. What was first incomprehensible suddenly becomes clear. The angels recall the words of Jesus and the prophecy of his Passion. Up to now these words seem to have been a dark memory for the disciples. Suddenly they begin to shine and illuminate the way to Jesus. All at once it becomes clear that Jesus had not only prophesied his death on the cross but his resurrection on the third day as well. The angel as interpreter, *angelus interpre,* has become an important image. The angels who accompany us lead us into the mystery of our life. They reveal meaning when everything seems meaningless. Without the right interpretation we cannot live right. We perceive our life based on our interpretation of it.

Parents are usually the interpreters of life for children. However, children often look for additional sources to bring meaning into their lives. A favorite source is grandparents, who interpret what the child senses from the standpoint of their own lives, bringing in another dimension. The mystery of life often shines through in their interpretation. This fascinates children and shows them that life has more to offer than the banality of everyday existence. Life is not only based on what is right and wrong, but has many dimensions that extend to the reaches of heaven. There are angels who accompany us and also let the wonder in our life shine through. Children are not satisfied with a purely superficial interpretation of life that offers conformity as the only possibility. Children want to feel the mystery of life and do not accept an interpretation that omits the subject of death. Only when death is not viewed as a catastrophe but as a means to resurrection are children satisfied. This is why they often have a more natural way of dealing with death than adults. Their angel tells them that death does not have the last word, but that the departed meet God in heaven and live there as the children have always imagined and wished life to be.

As adults, too, we always need angels to interpret our lives. In a conversation with a friend, we suddenly realize that there is a sense in everything we have experienced up to now and that God has been leading us on a good path. Or we hear a homily, and the meaning of the situation we are in at the moment suddenly becomes clear. We go home with a different feeling. We understand our life and can accept it the way it is. We attend a funeral and, like the women, go to the grave in deep mourning. There we sense meaning in the eulogy or pray, and that surrounds the situation with another light. Or we fail at something and complain to a friend about how our conception of life has been shattered. But after the conversation we sense that we are still able to carry on. We even discover a meaning in our failure. We see the people who interpret our destiny as angels. And we often perceive them as angels of resurrection who give us the gift of new trust to get up from our resignation and enter a new life.

24 The Angel Who Carries Us to Heaven (Lazarus)

The idea of the angel who comes to us when we die and bears us over the threshold of death exists in all nations. Researchers of life after death, such as Raimond Moody or Elisabeth Kübler-Ross, describe beings composed of light that appear to us in death and lovingly stand by our side. They speak about the angel accompanying us in the dying process and welcoming us into the next world. The image of the angel who accompanies us in death is taken up in the biblical story of the rich man and the poor man, Lazarus, who ill and covered with sores lay at the rich man's gate: "So it was that the beggar died, and was carried by the angels to Abraham's bosom" (Luke 16:22).

It is a widespread belief that we are carried to heaven by angels. When a funeral is held in my monastery and the coffin of a fellow brother is carried from the church to the cemetery, we sing the time-honored antiphon: "In paradisum deducant te angeli" ("May the angels accompany you to paradise"). The deceased shall be received by martyrs and be accompanied by them to the holy city of Jerusalem. The antiphon closes: "Chorus angelorum te suscipiat, et cum Lazaro quondam paupere aeternam habeas requiem" ("May the choir of angels receive you, and together with the once poor Lazarus, may you have eternal rest"). Here a reference is made to the story of the poor man Lazarus. The angels shall transport us to heaven just as they once did

Lazarus. Lazarus means: "God helps." In death, we are not without help. God himself sends his angels so that they will help us as well at the moment of death, when we are no longer able to help ourselves. The angels will carry us to the holy city in heaven, where angels and saints worship God. The choir of angels will rejoice when we arrive and sing a hymn of thanksgiving. There is a beautiful painting by an old master from the thirteenth century that shows the two archangels Raphael and Gabriel. They are carrying a departed soul, wrapped in a shroud, to heaven. It is an image of comfort for ill and dying people. They will not fall into the darkness of death, but will be carried by loving angels gently into the protective lap of God.

In the offertory of the funeral mass, Michael is praised as the angel who wants to lead us to eternal life. Following the prayer asking God to protect the faithfully departed from the torments of hell are the words: "May the standard-bearer Michael lead them to the shining light that You once promised Abraham and his successors." The liturgy continues to embrace the idea that angels will carry us to heaven. None other than the archangel Michael, the brave warrior of God, will fight for us, so that we arrive safely on the other shore, in the holy radiance of God where we are also transformed into light. It is a comforting image that an angel who has accompanied us during our life on earth, who has protected and encouraged us to truly live, who has healed our wounds and freed us from our prison, will also not abandon us in death. It will lead us safely over the abyss of death, the place that has always frightened people. Then our angel has fulfilled its mission and can forever take its place in the choir of angels singing the eternal praises of God in heaven. The angel does not leave us in our struggle with death. Through the presence of the angel, death loses its grip of terror. When we are helpless, at the mercy of pain and loneliness, the angel is by our side. We will not walk alone over the threshold of death, but in the company of our angel.

Johann Sebastian Bach concludes the chorus of the "Passion of St. John" with the consoling words:

> O Lord, in the final hour give leave to thy dear angels to convey my soul to the bosom of Abraham, the body resting gently in its peaceful chamber of sleep, devoid of torment and pain until the day of judgment. That my eyes may behold you in utter joy, O Son of God, my savior and throne of grace! Lord Jesus Christ hear my prayer for I will praise you eternally!

Although this language may be difficult for some to relate to, the near-death experiences many people report give a new meaning to these words. The angel of God will accompany us in death and transport us into God's loving arms. Children do not have a problem imagining this. They live in the world of the angel. And they are convinced that their angel will also carry them to the bosom of Abraham and that the place of death is in the motherly arms of God. Death is connected to birth and thus with the mother's womb. Here we will experience forever the protection that we have always yearned for. Though it is sensed here from time to time, these moments are fleeting and fragile. In death we will rest eternally in the motherly lap of God and, with the knowledge of God's love, enjoy everlasting happiness.

Conclusion

The angels whom the Bible tells us about show us that a healing closeness extends to all areas of our lives. God is not only the distant and incomprehensible mystery; God also affects our lives in a concrete way through angels. God sends us angels as people who accompany us for a time and open our eyes to true reality. God sends us angels in dreams to lead us in the right direction when we have come to a dead end, to provide our souls with the remedy they need to heal, and to break the chains that bind us. God comes to our aid through the angel in our hearts, in our thoughts, and in the quiet impulses felt in our soul. If we understand the theological view of angels as created spiritual beings, then God's healing closeness can be put into concrete terms and understood as a reality that has been created and can be experienced. God touches us through angels in the people we come into contact with, through moments of inspiration, and in dreams that leave a deep impression on our souls — one that we can examine and meditate on. This is a comforting message, a message that draws the distant and incomprehensible God into our everyday lives.

Everybody has an angel. This is the Good News of the biblical stories and the enlightenment passed down to us in our spiritual tradition. All people need a special place of protection and creative contemplation in the houses of their souls. This is where the angels who are with us live and where they lead us to the "effortlessness of being," to gentleness, love, and a desire for life. Angels inspire our souls. They lend wings to our fantasy, empowering it to rise above the banality of superficiality and to open heaven over the emptiness of our desert. The angel conveys to us the feeling that we are protected and secure in a special way. We are never alone. Angels accompany us in all the situations of our life: in loneliness, in the prison we find ourselves in, in fear, in depression, in the tomb of our self-pity, in resignation, in death. Angels will also carry us over the dark threshold of death and lead us to the light where we will sing with them the eternal hymn of praise to God.

Angels heard our cries as children when we were hurt or suffering, when we were at the mercy of erratic behavior and disrespect. Angels were with us in our pain, fear, and helplessness. From childhood, we have known about the angel at our side. We have also known about the angel as a source of the healing and protective forces inside us, inspiring our creative potential, providing us with a helpful idea and an inner resource that we could tap. Angels led us to the inner world where the pain of the outer world did not reach us. They conveyed to us an aura of dignity that no one could take away. As adults we can connect to the angel experiences we had in our childhood. However, this does not mean viewing our angel with the eyes of a child. We must see it in a mature and enlightened way. To perceive the angel in my own life means giving up my preoccupation with past hurt and suffering, my failure, and defeat. For me, coming into contact with the angel means discovering the angel tracks in my life.

In spiritual counseling I have often been able to witness how people experienced healing and liberation when they recognized the angel tracks in their lives and had a chance to meditate about them. Another power grew in them, a godly power. They came in contact with the place of the godly. And only in this place could they become the persons they were created to be. When they examined the angel in their lives, they were freed from the overbearing oppressiveness of hurtful and disrespectful people. Through the angel, they discovered God's healing and liberating closeness, God's loving and gentle breath, which blows through and envelopes every moment of their lives. The encounter with angels enables them to be angels for other people. And this seems to be the primary calling for all of us, to become the angel who opens heaven for other people and who conveys God's healing and loving closeness to them.

Works Cited

Bandini, Pietro. *Die Rückkehr der Engel: Von Schutzengeln, himmlischen Boten und der guten Kraft, die sie uns bringen* (The return of the angel: On guardian angels, heavenly messengers, and the good strength they bring to us). Bern, 1995.

Brückner, Annemarie. "Michaelsverehrung." In *Theologische Realenzyklopädie*, 22: 717–24.

Hark, Helmut. *Mit den Engeln gehen: Die Botschaft unserer spirituellen Begleiter* (Walking with angels: The message of our spiritual companions). Munich, 1993.

Jung, C. G. *Gesammelte Werke* (Collected works). Vol. 11, Zurich, 1963; vol. 13, Olten, 1978.

Kast, Verena. *Abschied von der Opferrolle* (Goodbye to the victim role). Stuttgart, 1998.

Stubbe, Ellen. *Die Wirklichkeit der Engel in Literatur, Kunst und Religion* (The reality of the angel in literature, art, and religion). Munster, 1995.

Vorgrimler, Herbert. *Wiederkehr der Engel? Ein altes Thema neu durchdacht* (Return of the angel: An old theme reassessed). Kevelaer, 1991.